A Survey of Transnational Corporations

Contents

Structures

Chapter 5 Intra-Company Trade and Transfer Pricing

5.1 Intra-Company Trade

5.2 Intra-Company Trade in America

5.2.1 Value of Intra-Company Trade of United States TNCs and Foreign TCNs in United States

5.2.2 Value of Trade Associated with United States TNCs

5.2.3 Composition of Intra-Company Trade

5.2.4 Intra-Company Trade's Relation to Trade Partners Income Level

5.3 Transfer Pricing

5.3.1 What is Transfer Price

5.3.2 How Does Transfer Price Reduce Total Tax Burden

5.3.3 Tax Avoidance

5.4 Tax Heavens and the Transnational Corporation

5.4.1 Types of Tax Heavens

5.4.2 How to Select the Type of Tax Heaven

Chapter 6 Strategies of Transnational Corporations

6.1 Traditional Method of Strategy Formulation

6.1.1 Environmental Analysis

6.1.2 Industry Analysis

6.1.3 Financial Analysis

6.1.4 Internal Diagnosis

6.2 Basic Strategies for Transnational Corporations

6.2.1 Generic Strategy

6.2.2 Competitive Strategy

Chapter 1
Introduction of Transnational Corporations

1.1 Name and Definition of Transnational Corporations

1.1.1 Name of Transnational Corporations

In the second half of the twentieth century, international business has become an important economic force. Today few, if any, countries are economically self-sufficient. In the developed countries, international business touches people's lives daily. If international business is the process of conducting business across national boundaries, then transnational corporations are the principal participants in this activity. They are, so to speak, the actors or players in the international business "game".

Transnational corporations are among the world's biggest economic institutions. A rough estimate suggests that the 300 largest TNCs own or control at least one-quarter of the entire world's productive assets, worth about US$5 trillion. TNCs' total annual sales are comparable to or greater than the yearly gross domestic product (GDP) of most countries (GDP is the total output of goods and services for final use by a nation's economy)

1.1. 2 Definition of Transnational Corporations

There is no single agreed-upon definition of the transnational corporations. This is because trans-nationality has many dimensions and can be viewed from several perspectives-economic, political, legal, etc.

1. Ownership Criterion:
Some argue that ownership is the key criterion. A firm

becomes transnational only when the headquarters or parent company is effectively owned by nationals of two or more countries. However, by ownership test, very few transnational corporations can be called transnational corporations.

2. Nationality Mix of Headquarters Managers:
An international company is transnational if the managers of the parent company are nationals of several countries. Usually, managers of the headquarters are nationals of the home country. This may be a traditional phenomenon. However, very few companies pass this test currently.

3. Business Strategy:
Generally speaking, it is to realize global profit maximization. Ethnocentric companies follow policies that are home country-oriented. Polycentric companies follow policies that are host country-oriented. Geocentric companies follow policies that are world-oriented.

An TNC is a parent company that (1) engages in foreign production through its affiliates located in several countries, (2) exercises direct control over the policies of its affiliates, (3) implements business strategies in production, marketing, finance and staffing that transcend national boundaries (geocentric).

A TNC can be a "public' corporation, which trades its shares of stock at stock exchanges or brokerage houses; the buyers from the public are "shareholders," and can include individuals as well as institutions such as banks, insurance companies, and pension funds. Or a TNC can be "private," meaning that it does not have shares which are traded publicly; such firms are frequently family-controlled.

A "parent" company, located in the TNC's country of origin, exercises an authoritative, controlling influence over a "subsidiary" in another country either directly if it is private or, if it is public, by owning some or all of the shares (parent corporations can exert controlling power even with relatively small share holdings in subsidiaries). Subsidiaries can have a different name than the parent company, and can of course also be located in the same country as the parent.

1. 2   Brief History of TNCs

1. 2.1   From the Origins to the Second World War

The earliest historical origins of transnational corporations can be traced to the major colonizing and imperialist ventures from Western Europe, notably England and Holland, which began in the 16th century and proceeded for the next several hundred years. During this period, firms such as the British East India Trading Company were formed to promote the trading activities or territorial acquisitions of their home countries in the Far East, Africa, and the Americas. The transnational corporation as it is known today, however, did not really appear until the 19th century, with the advent of industrial capitalism and its consequences: the development of the factory system; larger, more capital intensive manufacturing processes; better storage techniques; and faster means of transportation. During the 19th and early 20th centuries, the search for resources including minerals, petroleum, and foodstuffs as well as pressure to protect or increase markets drove transnational expansion by companies almost exclusively from the United States and a handful of

Western European nations. Sixty percent of these corporations' investments went to Latin America, Asia, Africa, and the Middle East. Fuelled by numerous mergers and acquisitions, monopolistic and oligopolistic concentration of large transnationals in major sectors such as petrochemicals and food also had its roots in these years. The US agribusiness giant United Fruit Company, for example, controlled 90 percent of US banana imports by 1899.

Demand for natural resources continued to provide an impetus for European and US corporate ventures between the First and Second World Wars. Although corporate investments from Europe declined somewhat, the activities of US TNCs expanded vigorously. In Japan, this period witnessed the growth of the zaibatsu (or "financial clique") including Mitsui and Mitsubishi. These giant corporations, which worked in alliance with the Japanese state, had oligopolistic control of the country's industrial, financial, and trade sectors.

1.2.2 From 1945 to the Present

US TNCs heavily dominated foreign investment activity in the two decades after the Second World War, when European and Japanese corporations began to play ever greater roles. In the 1950s, banks in the US, Europe, and Japan started to invest vast sums of money in industrial stocks, encouraging corporate mergers and furthering capital concentration. Major technological advances in shipping, transport (especially by air), computerization, and communications accelerated TNCs' increasing internationalization of investment and trade, while new advertising capabilities helped TNCs expand market shares.

All these trends meant that by the 1970s oligopolistic consolidation and TNCs role in global commerce was of a far different scale than earlier in the century. Whereas in 1906 there were two or three leading firms with assets of US$500 million, in 1971 there were 333 such corporations, one-third of which had assets of US$1 billion or more. Additionally, TNCs had come to control 70~80 percent of world trade outside the centrally planned economies.

Over the past quarter century, there has been a virtual proliferation of transnationals. In 1970, there were some 7,000 parent TNCs, while today that number has jumped to 38,000. The 90 percent of them are based in the industrialized world, which control over 207, 000 foreign subsidiaries. Since the early 1990s, these subsidiaries' global sales have surpassed worldwide trade exports as the principal vehicle to deliver goods and services to foreign markets.

The wealth of transnationals is concentrated among the top 100 firms which in 1992 had US$3.4 trillion in global assets, of which approximately US$1.3 trillion was held outside their home countries. The top 100 TNCs also account for about one-third of the combined outward foreign direct investment (FDD of their countries of origin. Since the mid-1980s, a large rise of TNC-led foreign direct investment has occurred. Between 1988 and 1993, worldwide FDI stock—a measure of the productive capacity of TNCs outside their home countries—grew from US$1.1 to US$2.1 trillion in estimated book value. There has also been a great increase in TNC investment in the less-industrialized world since the mid-1980s; such investment, along with private bank loans, has grown far more dramatically than national development aid or multilateral bank lending. Burdened by debt, low commodity prices, structural adjustment, and un-employment, governments throughout the less-industrialized world today view TNCs, in the words of the British magazine The Economist as "the embodiment of modernity and the prospect of wealth: full of technology, rich in capital, replete with skilled jobs." As a result, The Economist notes further, these governments have been "queuing up to attract multinationals" and liberalizing investment restrictions as well as privatizing public sector industries. For TNCs, less-industrialized countries offer not just the potential for market expansion but also lower wages and fewer health and environmental regulations.

Thus, in 1992 foreign investment into less-industrialized nations was over US$50 billion; the figure had jumped to US$71 billion in 1993 and US$80 billion in 1994. In 1992--1993, less-industrialized countries accounted for between one-third and two-fifths of global FDI inflows—more than at any time since 1970. These flows have not been evenly distributed, however, with just ten host recipients — the majority in Asia—accounting for up to 80 percent of all FDI to the less-industrialized world.

1.3   Problems Arising from TNCs

1.3.1.   Intra-Company Trade and Manipulative Price Transfers

The post-Second World War period witnessed not merely a rise in TNCs' control of world trade, but also growth of trade within related enterprises of a given corporation, or "intra-company" trade. While intra-company trade in natural resource products has been a feature of TNCs since before 1914, such trade in intermediate products and services is mainly a phenomenon of recent decades. By the 1960s, an estimated one-third of world trade was intra-company in nature, a proportion which has remained steady to the present day. The absolute level and value of intra-company trade has increased considerably since that time, however. Moreover, 80 percent of international payments for technology royalties and fees are made on an intra-company basis.

Problems stemming from intra-company trade concern TNCs' ability to maximize profits by avoiding both market mechanisms and national laws with an instrument of internal costing and accounting known as transfer pricing. This is a widespread technique whereby TNCs set prices for transfers of goods, services, technology, and loans between their worldwide affiliates which differ considerably from the prices which unrelated firms would have had to pay.

There are many benefits TNCs derive from transfer pricing. By lowering prices in countries where tax rates are high and raising them in countries with a lower tax rate, for example, TNCs can reduce their overall tax burden, thus boosting their overall profits. Virtually all intra-company relations including advisory services, insurance, and general management can be categorized as transactions and given a price; charges can as well be made for brand names, head office overheads, and research and development. Through their accounting systems TNCs can transfer these prices among their affiliates, shifting funds around the world to avoid taxation. Governments, which have no way to control TNCs' transfer pricing, are therefore under pressure to lower taxes as a means of attracting investment or keeping a company's operation in their country. Tax revenue which might be used for social programs or other domestic needs is thus lost.

Moreover, in countries where there are government controls preventing companies from setting product retail prices above a certain percentage of prices of imported goods or the cost of production, the firms can inflate import costs from their subsidiaries and then impose higher retail prices. Additionally, TNCs can use overpriced imports or underpriced exports to circumvent governmental ceilings on profit repatriation, causing nation-states to suffer large foreign exchange losses. For instance, if a parent company has a profitable subsidiary in a country where the parent does not wish to re-invest the profits, it can remit them by overpricing imports into that country. During the 1970s, investigations found that average overpricing by parent firms on imports by their Latin American subsidiaries in the pharmaceutical industry was 155 percent, while imports of dyestuffs raw materials by Indian TNC affiliates were being overpriced between 124 and 147 percent.

1.3.2   Influence in Nations' Political Affairs

TNCs' influence over countries, particularly those in the less-industrialized world, has not been manifest solely in sheer economic power or manipulative price transfers. Such influence has also been reflected in corporations' willingness and ability to exert leverage directly by employing government officials, participating on important national economic policy making committees, making financial contributions to political parties, and bribery. Furthermore, TNCs actively enlist the help of Northern governments to further or protect their interests in less-industrialized nations, assistance which has involved military force. In 1954, for instance, the US launched an invasion of Guatemala to prevent the Guatemalan government from taking (with compensation plus interest) unused land of United Fruit Company for redistribution to peasants.

Perhaps the most notorious example of TNCs' meddling in the political affairs of a sovereign state, however, occurred in the early 1970s, when International Telephone and Telegraph (ITT) offered the US Central Intelligence Agency US$1 million to finance a campaign to defeat the candidacy of Salvador Allende in Chilean national elections. Though this offer was refused, and Allende democratically elected, ITT continued to lobby the US government and other US corporations to promote opposition to Allende through economic pressure including the cutoff of credit and aid and support of Allende's political rivals. After copper mines in Chile owned by the firms Kennecott and Anaconda were nationalized, the US government took a series of steps based largely on the recommendations of ITT to subvert Allende.   of ITT's efforts to overthrow Allende helped prompt initiatives in the United Nations to draft a TNC Code of Conduct to establish some guidelines for corporate behavior. This move was part of more general concern about the extent of corporations' economic and political influence which emerged in the 1960s and 1970s, and which led some less-industrialized countries to demand that TNCs divest from certain sectors or to require changes in the terms of a company's investment. Yet such developments have been minor and temporary obstacles to the augmentation of TNCs economic power, and overall the past three decades have been characterized by increased regional economic integration, the liberalization of many international markets. and the opening up of new areas such as Central and Eastern Europe.

1. 4   TNCs and International Politics

Especially since the 1980s, TNCs' involvement at international political negotiations and fora has accompanied and encouraged the rise of global corporate economic power. In an effort to reduce barriers to trade and investment capital flows in the last decade, TNCs have lobbied vigorously to shape to their liking Europe's Single Market agreement, the North American Free Trade Agreement (NAFTA), and the Uruguay Round of the General Agreement on Tariffs and Trade (GATT). For TNCs, so-called free trade lessens governmental restrictions on their movement and ability to maximize returns. "The deregulation of trade aims to erase national boundaries insofar as these affect economic life," economists Herman Daly and Robert Goodland have noted. "The policy-making strength of the nation is thereby weakened, and the relative power of TNCs is increased.

For example, rules established in the GATT's concluded Uruguay Round regarding trade-related intellectual property rights (TRIPs) and trade-related investment measures (TRIMs) will be of particular benefit to TNCs. The first gives corporations greater capacity to privatize any patent life forms, including plant and other genetic resources of less-industrialized nations and peoples. TRIMs render illegal certain measures which countries have employed to encourage TNCs to establish linkages with domestic firms. TRIPs, TRIMs, and other GATT rules fall under the authority of the World Trade Organization (WTO), a new supranational body which works with the World Bank and other financial institutions to manage global economic policy to serve transnational corporate interests.

In another demonstration of transnationals' growing political might, and perhaps the most striking example to date of organized corporate lobbying on the world stage, TNCs' efforts at the 1992 United Nations Conference on Environment and Development (UNCED) in Rio de Janeiro undermined sections of the Summit's key documents. And well before the Summit took place. INC pressure had led to the removal from UNCED materials proposals to regulate the practices of global corporations.

1. 5   Effects of TNCs on Social Development

1. 5.1   Economic Growth

Transnational corporations can potentially promote social development through their activities that generate economic growth. One observer has written: "As per capita income increases, as levels of education increase and as the growth In communications technology increases awareness of alternative lifestyles, there are rising expectations with regard to matters such as housing, welfare, recreation, and medicine. These public welfare functions have traditionally been considered the province of public agencies."But as corporations are intimately involved with the growth of the economy, they are perceived by many as the most effective levers for change."

There exists some evidence that foreign direct investment by TNCs and the foreign exchange that TNCs provide can improve the economic performance of the countries in which they operate. "TNCs impact the process of economic growth by influencing the amount and quality of new capital formation, transfer of hard and soft technology, development of human resources, and the expansion of trade opportunities."

While in theory TNCs can promote social development by fostering economic growth, in practice this relationship rarely exists for two reasons. First, it is unclear whether transnational corporations are actually responsible for economic growth in host countries. In the most notable case of recent economic transformation, South Korea, transnational corporations played a negligible role. Furthermore, TNCs can actually hamper indigenous economic growth by driving local entrepreneurs out of business, importing key goods and services, remitting a majority of the profits to their home countries, and transferring fees and royalties to parent companies located outside the host economy.

Second, even if TNCs do improve a host country's economy, the relationship between economic growth and social development is tenuous. Although the global economy continues to grow annually, such growth is hardly curing problems of poverty, unemployment, disparities in wealth, or other issues of social malaise. In Cote D'Ivoire, for example, while TNCs might have helped to foster aggregate economic growth from 1960 to 1975, they did little to promote social development: unemployment increased, distribution of income widened and nationals increasingly lost control over the country's industrial capacities. In sum, while transnational corporations can be the engines of economic growth under some circumstances, the economic power of TNCs is rarely harnessed to achieve the ends of social development.

1. 5.2 Transfer of Technology

Transnational corporations can also indirectly affect social development through the transfer of technology to host countries. Transferred technology can assume many forms including hardware such as machinery and equipment; software such as blueprints; process and product design; and training in management, marketing and quality control methods. Furthermore, such technology can be transferred through a variety of methods including joint ventures, foreign direct investment, technical assistance, subcontracting arrangements and non-equity investments. TNC technology transfer can potentially provide host countries with a number of benefits, including enhanced economic growth. "More advanced foreign technology transfer has acted as a trigger mechanism for modern economic growth in some developing countries which are on a lower level of economic and social development. Technology transfer can advance economic growth in a variety of ways: facilitating the production of new goods with higher value-added content; increasing exports; increasing output for a given level of input; and improving management techniques. There also exists some evidence that transfers of technology can help develop a particular host country industry. For example, the expansion of foreign-owned TNC semiconductor plants off the coast of Singapore has spurred the emergence of the domestic semiconductor industry within Singapore itself.

TNC transfer of management skills can also potentially advance human resource development—an important component of social development. "Through its employment of indigenous professionals and managers, the multinational corporate subsidiary transmits knowledge and experiences that are less available locally." Transnational corporations can also foster human resource development through their research and development practices, particularly in developing countries. Such practices can potentially increase the skill levels and technical capabilities of employees in developing countries.

Although in theory transnational corporations can foster social development in developing countries by transferring management skills as well as research and development <R&D) capacities, in practice their record in this field is mixed. First, governments in developing countries have historically criticized TNCs for not employing enough nationals in management positions and, therefore, transferring only minimal management skills. Second, while large transnational corporations spend billions of dollars on research and development annually, they conduct only a small fraction of such R&D outside industrialized countries. Third, when transnational corporations do conduct R&D in developing countries, they often merely adapt existing technology to local conditions — a process that generates little impact on deeper indigenous research and innovation capabilities (know-why).

Finally, TNC transfer of technology policies in developing countries has received criticism on numerous other grounds. For example, there is some evidence that the technology transnational corporations transfer is too costly for developing countries, does not create local linkages, is protected too exclusively through patents, is often capital intensive and therefore inappropriate for labor-intensive developing countries, and produces goods for affluent classes while failing to meet local needs.

1.5.3   Transnational Corporations and Taxes

Transnational corporations can also indirectly foster social development through their provision of taxes to the state, because governments often use these revenues to finance social welfare programs. Such taxes can be substantial. For example, in 1989, foreign affiliates of US-based transnational corporations provided 15.5 per cent of government revenues in Guatemala, 12.2 per cent in Peru, and 4.6 per cent in Mexico. In 1992, Phillip Morris paid 4.5 billion dollars in taxes to the United States government alone, including billions more m employee and excise taxes.

While transnational corporations do pay substantial taxes under some circumstances, they engage in a variety of practices that intentionally deprive governments of tax revenues they are due. The ability of transnational corporations to move funds and goods rapidly between countries allows them to manipulate intra-company payments and avoid taxes—a process known as transfer pricing. For example, a German company manufacturing in France where tax rates are high sells its product at below-market values to a subsidiary in Puerto Rico where taxes are low. From Puerto Rico, the company sells to wholesalers or retailers, claiming a loss in France and huge profits in Puerto Rico where it pays minimal taxes. Countries have attempted to combat transfer pricing tactics through unitary taxation policies under which a government calculates a company's taxes on the basis of its global profits instead of on the basis of profit it declares within the country's borders. However, companies have successfully lobbied against unitary taxation policies in most jurisdictions.

Chapter 2
Formation of Transnational Corporations

2. 1   Transnational Operation of Corporation

2.1.1   The Location of Economic Activity

Some economic activity, by its very nature, must take place in close proximity to the markets which it serves. Most services must be rendered at the site of consumption. Other economic activity is more appropriately located nearer to sources of supply of the raw materials which are required as inputs in the final products. Under sufficiently competitive market conditions, commercial activity tends to locate relative to markets and input supplies where it can operate most profitably. Inappropriately located productive sites will yield lower returns or losses, and ultimately may result in failure and exit from the market.

In order to minimize the combination of production and shipping costs, products which lose weight in the manufacturing process tend to be produced closer to sources of supplies of the inputs of greatest weight per unit cost. Products which gain weight in the production process tend to be produced nearer to their final markets. Examples of weight-losing manufacturing processes are found in the re-finement of ores to produce metals of high purity. Any product which is assembled in stages from materials or components may serve as an example of a weight-gaining process.

2.1.2 Drives to Transnationalization

Virtually all multinational enterprises are large concerns (in terms of invested capital, sales volumes, number of employees, etc.) which operate in oligopolistic markets. They therefore possess varying amounts of monopoly power in the sense of being able to exercise pricing discretion. Their monopoly power is based upon either scale economies or superior knowledge which confers firm-specific competitive advantages. Such competitive advantage may be applied anywhere in the world, and thus can serve as the basis of a region-specific comparative advantage only at those sites where management chooses to establish operations.

If the benefits of scale economies or knowledge assets are sufficient to outweigh the costs of distance, cultural dif-ferences, and dealings with foreign governments, the man-agement of the multinational enterprise may expect greater income from operating in the foreign market than local firms can expect. To realize the larger incomes, the local firms would have to achieve comparable size (to exploit the economies of scale) or in some way acquire similar knowledge assets (which are costly to acquire). The reason that the multinational enterprise may be able to operate more economically in the foreign market than can local firms is that their knowledge assets were developed for the* home market", and thus are sunk costs; the marginal cost of development of the knowledge assets for the foreign market is therefore zero. But the marginal cost of acquiring such knowledge assets by local firms would be significantly non-zero. The exercise of superior knowledge by the multinational enterprise allows it to produce and sell differentiated products in the foreign market. This enables it to exercise monopoly pricing and capture economic rent for the knowledge assets.

A typical life cycle can be described for a product developed by a multinational enterprise. When the new product is introduced, production is initially retained in the home country (or where an affiliate first developed the new product) to allow close contact with design and production technical expertise. The product is sold in the domestic market and may be exported to foreign markets. However, as the product becomes standardized, the enterprise is able to shift production to affiliates in lower-cost foreign locales, most likely in other industrialized countries with large domestic and export markets so that scale economies can be exploited. A collateral phenomenon is that with standardization of the product, local firms can imitate the product (the competitive advantage of the superior knowledge assets begins to erode) to capture some of the multinational enterprise's export market. Foreign production at lower costs may then be a defensive measure undertaken by the multi-national enterprise in order to preserve market share.

In the latter stages of the product's life cycle, production in the multinational enterprise s home market may cease as the product continues to be available only as an import from its foreign affiliates. Continuing developments of new knowledge assets by the multinational enterprise are needed to sustain its home-country operations. It is in the continuing development of knowledge assets that the home country of the multinational enterprise may have its real comparative advantage.

The development of differentiated products and their sale in world markets is one means by which the multinational may be able to achieve an increased market share or a continually growing volume of sales. Competitor oligopolists are likely to feel compelled to follow a leader into international production and marketing as defensive measures in order to preserve their market shares. Such oligopolistic bunching of entry into foreign markets by competing multinational enterprises tends to be a common phenomenon.

Multinational enterprises may be more inclined to enter into foreign production of their products rather than exporting from the home country or licensing foreign producers. The reason is that by so doing they can internalize control of their superior knowledge assets and thereby protect them from erosion for a longer time. Because a newly developed superior knowledge tends to become a public good very quickly as others master or imitate it, the developer can capture an economic rent for it only as long as the knowledge is secret or can be held proprietary. Exporting the good from the domestic productive facilities, or licensing the production technology to foreign producers, tends to accelerate the deterioration of the proprietary nature of the knowledge assets. This may be regarded as an externality of market-organized transactions, i.e., the market price after the newly developed knowledge becomes a public good fails to reward the developer for the costs of developing the new knowledge. This market imperfection can be averted by the multinational enterprise by retaining sole proprietary exploitation of its superior knowledge assets within the firm and its foreign affiliates rather than letting the knowledge assets leak to the rest of the world through market transactions.

2. 2   Basic Pattern of TNCs' Formation

Now, we' ll describe the typical progression of an TNC from a home-based firm into one that enters multiple countries, in each country Sequentially adds lines of business, and within each line of business begins with limited functions and over time migrates to higher levels of functionality We'll also show that acquisitions may compress the process of formation, but typically do not change the basic pattern.

2. 2.1   Geographic Expansion

In recent years we have begun to see examples of firms that are "born transnational corporations" what from their birth have productive operations in more than one country. Yet these firms remain a distinct minority. The great majorities of transnational corporations begin in a home country and expand abroad through foreign market entry. The sequence by which firms expand from their home country into foreign markets is influenced by several factors, including geographic proximity, cultural similarity, and similarity in economic development.

1.   Geographic Proximity

The first location for foreign direct investment is often a neighboring country. Entering a neighbor country is a natural first step, as the firm can more easily identify market opportunities and gather vital information about competitive reactions and government policies in a nearby country than in a distant one. Firms may also prefer to enter neighboring countries first, as the cost of communicating with the foreign subsidiary is lower once the firm has expanded into nearby countries it may then move sequentially into countries that are farther away, minimizing the incremental distance of each move. Over time, through this process of entry based on geographic proximity, the firm can achieve a broad international position.

2. Cultural Similarity

The sequence of geographic expansion may also reflect cultural similarity between the transnational corporations home country and the host country. Success in a foreign country requires an understanding of local customs and consumer habits; effective communication with customers, suppliers, and employees; and good relations with govern-mental bodies. For all these reasons, firms often prefer to enter countries that are relatively similar in culture, i.e., where the "psychic distance" is low As they gain experi-ence in countries that are relatively similar to their own, transnational corporations learn how to manage outside their home country and may subsequently enter countries that are progressively less similar. Eventually, they may be able to enter countries that are at a considerable "psychic distance" from their country of origin.

3. Similarity in Economic Development

The level of host country economic development also

affects the choice of which markets to enter. Transnational corporations are often attracted to foreign markets where consumer buying habits and levels of disposable income are similar to those of home market consumers. In such markets, the TNC's product formulation and its marketing approach may require only modest adaptation. As the transnational corporation learns how to compete effectively in foreign markets of similar economic standing, it develops capabilities that may allow it to enter increasingly different foreign markets.

Geographic proximity, cultural similarity, and similarity in economic development can be understood in terms of organizational learning and capability development. In each instance, firms first expand into countries where the capabilities developed in their home market are most likely to be successful, and defer entry into countries where success is less likely. Accumulating experience in initial foreign markets enables the firm to develop new capabilities, which allow it to expand into countries that are more distant and less similar. TNC geographic expansion is not merely the sequential exploitation of existing capabilities in markets that are progressively farther from home, but the development of new capabilities as well.

2. 2. 2 Line of Business Diversification

Whereas some TNCs are single-business firms, most compete in more than one line of business. Foreign subsidiaries for such firms often begin by competing in one or a few of the parent s lines of business, over time adding more lines of business, and eventually operating in many or all of the parent's businesses. For many TNCs, then, line of business diversification represents a second dimension of evolution. Interestingly, there has been relatively little research into line of business diversification within foreign subsidiaries. It has been more common to speak of "the country subsidiary" as if it were monolithic, yet it is clear that most TNCs ramp up their activities over time, rather than entering in all lines of business at once.

In what sequence do foreign subsidiaries add lines of business? A recent study of Japanese electronics firms in the United States from 1976 to 1989 showed a sequential pattern of entry, beginning with lines of business that enjoyed the greatest advantage over local firms. By choosing their strongest line of business, these firms could offset the disadvantages they faced due to lack of familiarity with the local market and its competitive environment. As the subsidiary gained experience in doing business locally, it could add lines of business that enjoyed lower competitive advantage. Finally, when the TNC learned to compete effectively in the local environment it could add lines of business that offered little or no competitive advantage, but that sought to learn from technologically superior U. S. firms. Several subsidiaries of Japanese electronics firms added lines of business in precisely this fashion, adding new lines of business only when confident of success.

Of course, a line of business diversification does not happen automatically, but is driven by an intra-firm decision process of evaluation, action, monitoring, and further action. At each step, the firm must determine if the benefits of adding new lines of business are sufficient to offset disadvantages faced in the local market. Over time, as local expertise is accumulated and the subsidiary offers a strong infrastructure for country management, the firm may become increasingly confident of its ability to add new lines of business- With each successive entry the firm adds to its resources: it develops a reputation as a good employer and as a good customer for local supplier, it earns about local regulations, and in general it accumulates capabilities that make it possible for the firm to enter additional lines of business. Entry into these later lines of business might only be possible because of a strong country organization, which can provide management support, financial infrastructure, and technical expertise to new lines of business.

2.2.3   Functional Migration

Functional migration speaks to the development of activities performed by lines of business within a country. Some TNCs tended first to export to foreign markets, then to set up foreign sales subsidiaries to manage these imports, and eventually to establish wholly owned subsidiaries. Once established, lines of business typically continue to perform functions in their home country that lent themselves to economies of scale, such as R&D, product design, and strategic leadership. They performed in the host country only those functions that called for local knowledge, typically marketing and distribution. Over time, however, the subsidiary may take on additional functions, including assembly, local design, and procurement. In some instances, when the subsidiary develops worldwide expertise in the line of business, it may take on the role of business planning and even strategic leadership. In other instances, subsidiaries establish particular functions that serve as "centers of excellence "for the TNC.

The process of functional migration is seen most clearly in Greenfield investments, where subsidiaries begin with a limited number of functions and add new ones incrementally. Entry through acquisition quite naturally exhibits a different pattern. If the TNC acquires a local firm that is vertically integrated, it effectively bypasses the process of functional migration and gains all functions in a single step. Very often, however, TNCs enter a foreign market by acquiring a local company that performs some but not all functions. For example, some TNCs acquire local firms in order to gain an established distribution network through which they can sell imported products. Initial functions are acquired rather than set up from scratch, but subsequent functions-including assembly and products design are added over time. In other instances, firms may enter a foreign market with a Green-field investment, and then add functions through the acquisition of local firms Examples include the acquisition of manufacturing capacity' especially attractive when the industry has considerable excess capacity and building a new plant makes little sense) or the acquisition of a local R&D lab. Thus, acquisitions may differ from Greenfield investments in that they accelerate functional migration, yet they typically do not alter the basic sequence.

Migrating to higher levels of functionality faces a shifting set of impediments At early steps, which usually involve the location of assembly or manufacturing activities in the new subsidiary the most important impediments frequently involve the effective transfer of technical know-how and the ability to secure resources locally Later stages encounter very different — and sometimes more severe-obstacles, as the objective is not merely to replicate existing functions in a foreign market, but actually to shift functions from the home county to a foreign subsidiary — Such a shift may trigger resistance from home county managers, making evolution to higher functions a very difficult matter.

2. 3   Features of TNCs ' Formation Process

The hallmark of an TNC is that its dimensions are not separate and unrelated, but that they are interconnected. The ability to leverage knowledge across and among dimensions is precisely what gives TNCs their most compelling advantage. Accordingly, evolution along one dimension should not disregard evolution along other dimensions, but should affect, and be affected by, changing activities elsewhere in the firm. Without such integration, the TNC may exhibit substantial duplication, both among lines of business and also of functions within lines of business.

2.3.1   Integration of the Three Patterns

Learning about doing business in foreign countries helps further geographic expansion, learning about a given host country enables a sequential line of business addition in that country and so forth. Of course, experience gained by a line of business in one country not only leads to greater knowledge of that country it can also lead to greater knowledge of the line of business, which can be leveraged across countries to speed up the entry of that business in other countries. In this way, leveraging knowledge across dimension results in evolution that is faster and more extensive at any point in time than it would otherwise have been. Functional migration can also be accelerated by knowledge of particular functions accumulated across lines of business in the same country. For instance, it may be difficult for the first line of business in a country to undertake a new function, such as local parts procurement, product design, or strategic planning. Once the first line of business has successfully added that function, its experience can be leveraged to other lines of business in the same country, helping speed up their migration to the same level of functionality. Similarly, functional knowledge can be leveraged across countries to accelerate functional migration elsewhere in the world.

2. 3. 2 Skipping Development

Leveraging knowledge among dimensions of a TNC can also lead to development that is discontinuous, or that skips steps. This can take place along each of the three dimensions. Along each dimension the notion is the same: by identifying and taking advantage of economies of scale and scope, firms may be able to share capabilities across dimensions, obviating the need to perform every step. The result is a more efficient development, as the firm maximizes the salutary effects of scale and scope economies. TNCs may evolve in a discontinuous manner, skipping functions in given lines of business, skipping lines of business in some countries, or even deciding not to enter particular countries at all. TNCs that evolve in a punctuated manner will exhibit a pattern of development that is irregular and asymmetrical, but that achieves a minimum of duplication and therefore secures a greater level of efficiency.

Assume that a line of business within a subsidiary performs a variety of functions. If a new line of business is added, that line of business can make use of functions already performed by existing lines of business and avoid having to perform them. TNCs may also be able to share functions across countries within a single line of business. For instance, if one line of business performs manufacturing at a sufficient capacity to serve a neighboring country as well, the line of business in the neighboring country may not need to perform any manufacturing. Similarly the presence of a strong R&D lab in one country may obviate the need for a subsidiary in another country to perform its own R&D.

If all functions in a given line of business offer economies of scale, it might be unnecessary to perform any functions of that line of business in a second country. In that event, there would be no need to add that line of business in a second country since the second country could be served by the first for that line of business. If we extend this logic one step further, it could be that all lines of business can serve a neighboring country, making it unnecessary to establish a subsidiary in that country at all. Examples of this kind are increasingly common the European Union, where the establishment of a subsidiary in one EU country may enable a firm to operate in other EU countries without setting up separate subsidiaries.

2. 3.3   Restructuring the Worldwide Operations

In recent years, as global competition has intensified due to a convergence of consumer demand, increasing op-portunities for economies of scale and scope, and rising levels of industrialization around the word, many TNCs have begun to restructure their worldwide operations. In some instances they have consolidated existing functions and lines of business, and in other instances have shut down entire subsidiaries.

Regarding firm factors, the potential for efficiencies through global restructuring might be most common in TNCs that expanded many years ago. Because dose coordination of foreign subsidiaries was retentively difficult, older TNCs were frequently organized on a country-by-country basis and pursued a multi-domestic strategy. These TNCs often preformed all functions in each line of business, resulting in a high level of duplication among countries. Recently, because of enhanced global communications and transportation, opportunities have arisen to capture greater scale and scope economies, leading to a consolidation of functions among lines of business, as well as a consolidation of lines of business among country subsidiaries. The pressure for restructuring is also likely to be greater in global industries, where competition on a global scale imposes an imperative for worldwide efficiency. As firms in an industry begin to manage their activities on a worldwide basis, other firms will face an imperative to do likewise. Taking these points together, TNCs that are most likely to restructure their ac- tivities are those that expanded abroad long ago and now find themselves in highly global industries.

The process is difficult, as there is natural resistance within the firm to restructuring and consolidation, yet the end result is similar to the former: an asymmetrical mix of functions in each line of business, a varying set of lines of business in each country and even an irregular set of sub- sidiaries around the word.

Chapter 3
Foreign Direct Investment

3. 1 Definition and Types of Foreign Direct Investment

FDI is, in essence, the creation or expansion of firms that operate across national boundaries. Direct investment is an integral part of large firms overall strategy for global production and sales. These firms are the transnational enterprises which serve as the largest sources of FDI and foremost agents of FDI growth in the global economy.

3.1.1 Definition of FDI

Foreign direct investment (FDI) occurs when an investor based in one country (the home country) acquires an asset in another country (the host country) with the intent to manage that asset. It is the "management with control" of the asset that is significant in FDI and distinguishes the latter from portfolio investment in foreign stocks, bonds and other financial instruments. In most instances, both the investor and the asset it manages abroad are business firms. In such cases, the investor is typically referred to as the "parent firm" and the asset as the "affiliate" or "subsidiary". Not too long ago, most transnational corporations were big, but increasingly small and medium-sized enterprises am engaging in FDI.

3.1.2 Types of FDI

There are a variety of ways that FDI can occur, including

building new foreign facilities from scratch ("Greenfield Investment"), merging with a foreign firm, taking over a foreign firm, and entering a partnership with a foreign firm (for example, a joint venture). In general, there are three main categories of FDI:

1. Equity capital is the value of the TNC s investment in shares of an enterprise in a foreign country. An equity capital stake of 10 per cent or more of the ordinary shares or voting power in an incorporated enterprise, or its equivalent in an unincorporated enterprise, is normally considered as a threshold for the control of assets. This category includes both mergers and acquisitions and the creation of new facilities, often termed "Greenfield Investments". Mergers and acquisitions are an important source of FDI for developed countries, although the relative importance varies considerably.

2. Reinvested earnings are the TNC s share of affiliate earnings not distributed as dividends or remitted to the TNC. Such retained profits by affiliates are assumed to be reinvested in the affiliate. This can represent up to 60 percent of outward FDI in countries such as the United States and the United Kingdom.

3. Intra-Company Borrowing and Lending: This constitutes long-and short-term borrowing and lending of funds between the TNC and the affiliate.

The three main types of FDI, as described above, are collected by national statistical agencies and are reflected in the balance of payments statistics by IMF (WTO. 1996).

However, comprehensive and   data on FDI is yet to be recorded consistent in all countries,   which   makes conclusions to bed drawn from any study on FDI flows difficult.

In addition, FDI can also be divided into two other types: Horizontal FDI and Vertical FDI. Horizontal FDI involves investing in a firm that is in the same industry. Vertical FDI involves investing in a supplier or customer firm.

3.2   The Importance of FDI

There are many reasons why foreign direct investment (FDI) has become a much-discussed topic. One is the dramatic increase in the annual global flow between 1985 and 1995, from around $60 billion to an estimated $315 billion, and the resulting rise in its relative importance as a source of investment funds for a number of countries. Stocks of FDI, in turn, have been growing and estimates suggest that the sales of foreign affiliates of transnational corporations (TNCs) exceed the value of world trade in goods and services (the latter was S6100 billion in 1995), that intra-firm trade among TNCs accounts for about one-third of world trade, and that TNC exports to non-affiliates account for another third of world trade, with the remaining one-third accounted for by trade among national (non-TNC) firms.

The keen interest in FDI is also part of a broader interest in the forces propelling the ongoing integration of the world economy, or what popularly described as "globalization". Together with the more or less steady rise in the world's trade-to-GDP ratio, the increased importance of foreign-owned production and distribution facilities in most countries is cited as tangible evidence of globalization.

Foreign direct investment is a so viewed as a way of increasing the efficiency with which the world's scarce resources are used. A recent and specific example is the perceived role of FDI in efforts to stimulate economic growth in many of the world's poorest countries. Partly this is because of the expected continued decline in the role of development assistance (on which these countries have traditionally relied heavily), and resulting search for alternative sources of foreign capital. FDI, very little of which currently flows to the poorest countries, can be a source not just of badly needed capital, but also new technology and intangibles such as organizational and managerial skills, and marketing networks. FDI can also provide a stimulus to competition, innovation, savings and capital formation, and through these effects, to job creation and economic growth. Along with major reforms in domestic policies and practices in the poorest countries, this is precisely what is needed to turn-around an otherwise pessimistic outlook.

At an institutional level, the growing importance of FDI, coupled with the absence of binding multilateral rules on national policies toward FDI, has created what in many quarters is viewed as an obstacle that could slowdown the pace of further integration of the world economy. The perceived need for multilateral rules on investment is not new—indeed, the Havana Charter for the stillborn International Trade Organization (origin of the GATT and "spiritual ancestor" of the WTO) contained provisions on foreign investment—but attempts to reach a comprehensive multilateral agreement with binding rules have thus far not been successful.

Renewed interest in FDI within the trade community has been stimulated by the perception that trade and FDI are simply two ways—sometimes alternatives, but increasingly complementary—of servicing foreign markets, and that they are already interlinked in a variety of ways.

3.3 Trade and FDI Linkages

Trade and FDI are interrelated activities. Two sets of links are highlighted in the literature. The first is the impact of trade policies on FDI. The pattern of trade and trade policies may influence the size, direction and composition of the FDI flows. Trade policies, such as tariff barriers, can, for example, serve as incentives to FDI inflows, either as a deliberate act of policy or inadvertently. An interest in jumping a high tariff, for instance, can induce foreign direct investment in the local market. Other import barriers, quantitative limits on imports in a particular sector, could also induce FDI in the form of expanded production in the local market. Regional (or in some case global) trade agreements and economic integration may also influence FDI decisions by firms. Larger market size, resulting from regional trade agreements, provides opportunities for investors to take advantage of economies of scale, and, therefore, encourage investment flows. Rules of Origin, which distinguish between products produced by countries party to the regional agreement and those that are not, also may include third country investment.

The second set of links is the impact of FDI on trade. FDI policies by affecting investment decisions influence the size, direction and composition of trade and subsequently its contribution to growth and development. FDI can have sweeping and dynamic effects on the host country as it stimulates capital formation, competition, innovation, productivity and savings. All these factors can impact on a country's import and export activities. Several studies, covering a number of sectors, confirm a positive relationship between FDI inflows in the host country and the total volume of a host country's exports.

Moreover, there is some evidence to suggest that in general, foreign-owned firms have a higher propensity to export than locally-owned firms. Foreign firms often have a better knowledge of the international market and can more quickly respond to changing international demands. The size and efficiency of their distribution network may also give foreign firms an advantage. Several studies also show that foreign affiliates can have a positive spillover impact on the export propensity of local firms. Export performance may also be encouraged through FDI policy. Investment policies, such as those seeking to impose a mandatory requirement to export a certain portion of the local production and/or FDI policy biased towards export-oriented sectors, are designed with export promotion in mind.

The evidence on the relationship between FDI and imports is mixed. Some studies indicate that the inflow of FDI reduces host country's imports. Other studies find that inward FDI raises host country's import levels. Affiliates normally have a high propensity to import intermediate inputs from the home country, particularly when such inputs are either not available in the host country or the quality of the local supplies is not assured.

3. 4   Measurement of FDI

The available statistics on FDI. Which are far from ideal, come mainly from three sources First, mere are statistics from the records of ministries and agencies which administer the country's laws and regulations on FDI. The request for a license or the fulfillment of notification requirements allows these agencies to record data on FDI flows. Typically, re-invested earnings, intra-company loans, and liquidations of investment are not recorded, and not all notified investments are fully realized n the period covered by notification. Second, there are the FDI data taken from government and other surveys which evaluate financial and operating data of companies. While these data provide information on sales (domestic and foreign), earnings, employment and the share of value added of foreign affiliates in domestic output, they often are not comparable across countries because of differences in definitions and cover- age. Third, there are the data taken from national balance-of-payments statistics, for which internationally agreed guidelines exist in the fifth edition of the IMF Balance of Payments Manual. The three main categories of FDI described above are those used in balance-of-payments statistics.

At present, many countries have not yet fully implemented the IMF guidelines (in particular, re-invested earnings and inter-company transactions are not always covered), which impairs the comparability of FDI data across countries. In addition, a large number of developing countries do not provide FDI data. UNCTAD's 1995 World Investment Report had to rely on OECD partner statistics to estimate FDI flows for about 55 economies. Despite recent improvements, more efforts at the national level are needed before comparable and reasonably comprehensive FDI data will be available at the global level.

3. 5 Motives for Foreign Direct Investment

Foreign direct investment occurs because of "market imperfection." Market imperfections are departures from the assumptions of 1) Perfect competition (large number of firms, standardized goods, all information freely available, etc.); 2) No barriers to trade; 3) No transactions costs, transportation costs, taxes, etc.

There are five categories of motives for FDI.

1. Firm-specific (first mover) advantages

When we discussed trade theory, the term "first-mover advantages" was used to describe the competitive advantages of countries. The term "firm-specific advantage" is used to describe the competitive advantage of firms. They include the economies of scale, production know-how, marketing skills, brand reputation, managerial ability, and so forth.

The existence of firm-specific advantages is a form of market imperfection. Firm-specific advantages arise because products are not standardized and information is not freely available. Firm-specific advantages create barriers to entry for competitors.

Why do firm-specific advantages prompt FDI? A firm does not want to share its firm-specific advantages. It is best off if it can exploit them itself. Thus, for example, a firm that has exclusive knowledge of a technology will want to do its own production for a foreign market rather than licensing the technology to another firm, which has every incentive to then steal the idea.

2. Internalization

Some investments are motivated by the desire to minimize

uncertainty by putting two firms under common control. This is most easily seen by considering vertical FDI. A firm that acquires control of a supplier (examples: an aluminum smelter that buys an aluminum mining firm, a computer manufacturer that buys a semiconductor maker) removes a great deal of uncertainty about the availability and price of supplies. Similarly, a firm that invests in a customer removes uncertainty about demand for its product.

3. Oligopolistic Behavior

An oligopoly is a market structure with a small number of firms. The key feature is that the number is so small that each firm bases its decisions on what its competitors are doing or are expected to do. This is different than the market structure we call perfect competition, in which there is such a large number of firms that no one firm can affect the market, and hence there is no need to pay attention to competitors' decisions.

When FDI is motivated by the actions or probable actions of competitors, this is oligopolistic behavior. For example, a firm might seek to invest abroad because its competitors are investing abroad. Alternatively, the firm may view foreign investment as a way to preempt its competitors' moves into a foreign market.

4. Inherent Locational Advantages

A locational advantage is a factor that pulls a firm to invest in a particular location. In contrast, one could view the previous three factors (firm-specific advantages, internalization and oligopolistic behavior) as push factors. (Note: Do not confuse the term "locational" with localization". These are different concepts. As seen below, localization could be a reason for a locational advantage.)

An inherent locational advantage refers to some natural feature of the particular foreign location. It could be related to geography. For example, the foreign investment could be motivated by a desire to minimize transportation costs or a desire to be close to customers so as to minimize distribution and service costs.

Being close to customers could also facilitate adaptation of the product or service to local market conditions and consumer preferences ("localization"). Access to resources provides another set of inherent locational advantages. The draw could be low-cost labor, skilled labor, R&D facilities, cheap energy, mineral resources, etc.

5.   Policy-Driven Locational Advantages

Policy-driven locational advantages are created by government policies that either push or pull firms into foreign investments. Trade barriers can be a powerful push factor. High actual (or potential) barriers to export make it attractive for a firm to produce within the market, and thus avoid the trade barriers altogether. Much of the Japanese investment in automobile manufacturing in the U.S. can be explained by voluntary export restraints and the threat of U.S. trade remedy laws.

Government inducements for foreign investors create a pull factor. Many governmental units offer incentives such as tax breaks, infrastructure investments, and subsidized land and utility costs in an effort to attract foreign investors. Governments also serve as information providers, and try to match potential investors with specific locations or local firms. Host country policies regarding FDI can be rather schizophrenic, with the national government imposing restrictions   (e. g. for national security reasons) and local governments providing incentives (in order to attract jobs and tax revenue).

Chapter 4
The Organization and Management of Transnational Corporations

4. 1   Introduction

How companies organize activities-research and development, production, marketing, and service, among others often means the difference between failure and success. Organization decisions ultimately focus on how activities are configured and coordinated. Configuration pertains to the geography positioning of activities and is driven by a company's interest in accessing markets and sources of comparative advantage. Activities range from being "concentrated" (i. e., each activity is located in a single country from which the worried is served), or "dispensed" (i.e., all activities are located in each host country) in contrast, coordination pertains to the integration or interdependence of activities, and is driven by a company's interest in exploiting competitive advantages across countries. Coordination ranges from very low, where each activity of a business is performed independently, to very high. Where the same activities are tightly coordinated or linked across geographical locations. How a company configures and coordinates its activities directly impacts its ability to exploit country-specific comparative advantages as well as company specific competencies.

An important point to remember is that there is no one best organizational design. The choice of an organizational design depends mostly on the choice of strategy. That is some design options are more effective for implementing different strategies. In addition, the choice of design options depends on the firm's resources. To modify an organizational design successfully requires that companies have the necessary personnel to staff newly created organization. For companies operating internationally, as you will see here, the key issue is the degree to which a company has a local responsiveness or globe strategic orientation.

4.2 Common International Organization Structures
4.2.1   International Division Structure

Much of the early work on international organization structures took the logical approach of relating the structure to the growth of a company's international activity. A company for example, might begin with an export department to handle the technical requirements of shipping products across national borders. With success in export markets would come a greater awareness of international opportunities, and the next organizational stage might be the establishment of an international division to look after both exports and foreign investments. The organization structure of a company with an international division might appear as shown in Exhibit 4-1.

Under an international division structure, all functional activities, with the possible exception of sales, are maintained at home. When international sales and profits are a minor percentage of a division's overall activity it is difficult to get a busy division manager to spend time cultivating and building international activity. Time tends to get spent where the big sales and profits are. Building and cultivating are best done by a division devoted exclusively to that task-hence the international division. One clear advantage of an international division structure is that it allows a company to give international sales much greater support and attention. As a result, the manager of the international division has to understand the product-market strategies of each product division and adapt them to international markets.

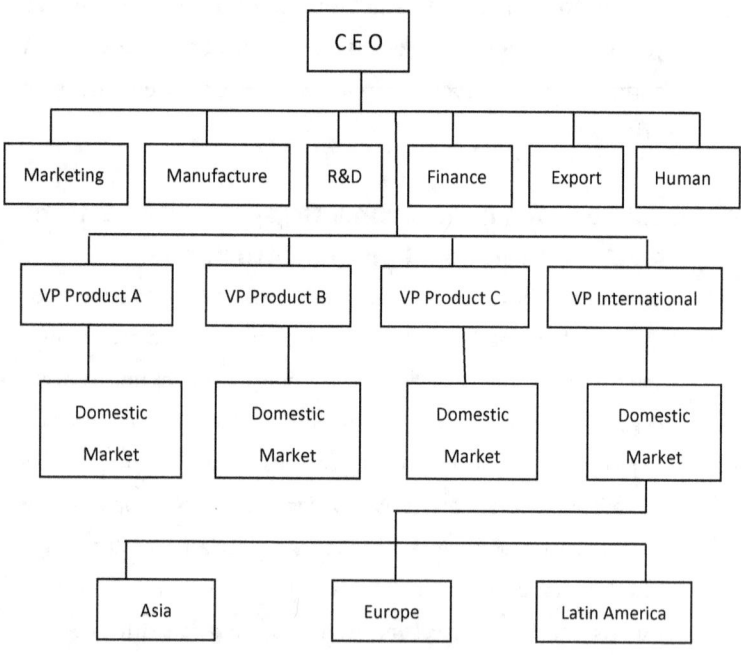

Exhibit 4-1   The International Division Structure

4. 2.2   Area Division Structure

As international sales grow as a percentage of total company sales, many successful companies evolve out of an international division structure and create an area division structure (Exhibit 4-2). While an area division will often continue to report to a corporate vice president international, strategic decision making is shifted to regional and/or country managers. As a result, the position of vice president international is one of the few positions in business where success can bring declining influence.

For many companies, area division structures capture the majority of efficiency advantages that result from global-ization. Relatively few activities actually require global volumes to reach maximum levels of economic efficiency. Furthermore, area organizations may be more efficient and effective than global structures because of increased responsiveness, reduced bureaucracy, communication efficiencies, and improved employee morale. In many cases area structures can facilitate faster delivery, allow greater customization, and require smaller inventories than would be possible under more complex organization forms.

Exhibit 4-2   The Area Division Structure

Under an area division structure, regional and country managers have a high degree of autonomy in how they adapt the strategies of the home country product divisions to meet the particular circumstances of their regions and countries.

The more local conditions influence consumer demand, the more autonomy country managers usually get. Local responsiveness is its main achievement. As a result, an area division structure is most appropriate for companies pursuing multi-domestic strategies.

Under an area division structure, the majority of activities are 'dispersed', or located in each country where the company competes. At Shell oil, for example, major refineries are located throughout almost all of the major markets of the world; crude oil purchasing activities are dispersed; and marketing and sales activities are also positioned around the world. Under an area division structure, these dispersed activities are loosely coordinated. This means that each activity is performed independently. For Shell oil, purchasing decisions made in the United States are not coordinated with purchasing decisions made in France or Indonesia.

4. 2. 3   Global Product Divisions

As a general rule, the relative importance of product managers increases with the number of products being offered by a company. As the diversity of foreign products increases, many successful companies have adopted global product division structures. DuPont became the first major U. S. company to adopt a modern-divisionalized structure not long after the turn of the century. By 1970, as many as 90 percent of Fortune 500 companies had adopted product divisional structures.

Divisions are usually organized to correspond to particular industries, or industry segments. U. K. -based Hanson PLC has 12 major divisions, each confronting substantially different industry pressures: Jacuzzi, Smith Corona, Imperial Tobacco, Farberware, Ames, Grove Crane, London Brick, Kaiser, SCM Chemicals, Universal Gym, British Ever Ready, and Ground Round. Other TNCs including ITT, Bayer, General Electric, Sandoz, Grand Metropolitan, Philip Morris, and Eastman Kodak—have highly diversified operations that lend themselves to distinct industry analyses and diverse business unit strategies. Under a divisionalized structure, all functional activities (for example, R&D, production, marketing) are controlled by a product group. An example of a global product divisional structure is included in Exhibit 4-3.

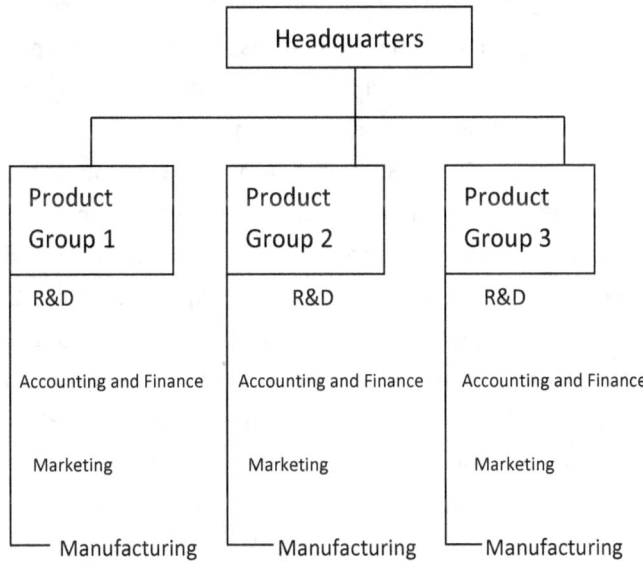

Exhibit 4-3   Global Product Structure

When global product divisions take over, they tend to

achieve direct lines of communication into key markets and can therefore get their product and market know-how through to the field unimpeded. Because the head office tightly coordinates activities country managers are often involved only in the local administrative, legal, and home country managers make financial affairs of the company product decisions and input from overseas affiliates is often discouraged. What is lost in terms of local responsiveness is gained in terms of global efficiencies.

Global product division structures represent a chain of vertically integrated activities. Product division managers can configure activities according to variances in costs or skills across countries. This makes the product divisions ideal for global strategies. Under a global product division structure, some activities may be dispersed—for example, component manufacturing and assembly—while others may be centrally located—for example, research and development. For U.S. and European companies, the advantages of global structural flexibility have become increasingly apparent through the growing international success of Japanese TNCs. In an attempt to drive costs down, a frequent reaction for U.S. and European companies has beer to move labor-intensive upstream activities to low-wage countries with highly skilled workers and duty-free zones. Many of these factories ended up in the Far East and, for American companies, in Mexico.

One of the reasons that many large companies have shifted to global product division structures is because it helps manager's focus more easily on maximizing competitiveness. When the competitive domain is set by industry boundaries, competitors can be clearly identified and decisions focused on upgrading functional skills. With rising globalization, plants can be more easily focused in terms of product, robotized in terms of technology, and diversified in terms of markets served. Country managers whose chief expertise is knowledge of their domestic markets cannot expect to survive globalization with their autonomy intact.

4.2.4   The Worldwide Matrix Structure

To balance the benefits produced by geographic and product structures and to coordinate a mixture of product and geographic subunits, some transnationals create a worldwide matrix structure. Unlike most hybrid organization: It has matrix provides the structure for a firm to pursue both local and more global strategies at the same time. Geographical divisions focus on national responsiveness, and product divisions focus on finding global efficiencies. The matrix structure works well only when there are nearly equal demands from the environment for local adaptation and for product standardization with its associated economies of scale. Without these near-equal demands, the organization tends to evolve into a product or geographic structure, based on which side is more important for competitive advantage.

In theory, the matrix produces quality decisions because two or more managers reach consensus on how to balance local and worldwide needs. Managers who hold positions at the intersection of product and geographic divisions are called "two-boss managers' as they have a boss from the product side of the organization and a boss from the geographic side of the organization product bosses tend to emphasize goals such as efficiency and using worldwide products, while geographic bosses tended to balance globalization and localization pressures. As such, for managers at all levels, the matrix requires continuously compensating for product needs and geographical needs.

To succeed at balancing the inherent struggles between global and local concerns, the matrix requires extensive resources for communication among the managers. Middle and upper-level managers must have good human-relations skills to deal with inevitable personal conflicts originating from the competing interests of product and geography. The middle-level managers must also learn to deal with two bosses, who often have competing interests. Upper-level managers, in turn, must be prepared to resolve conflicts between geographic and product managers.

Is the matrix worth the effort? During the 1980s the matrix structure was a popular organizational solution to the global-local dilemma. More recently, however, the matrix has come under fire because consensus decision making between product and geographic managers has proved slow and cumbersome. In many organizations, the matrixes became too bureaucratic, with too many meetings and too much conflict.

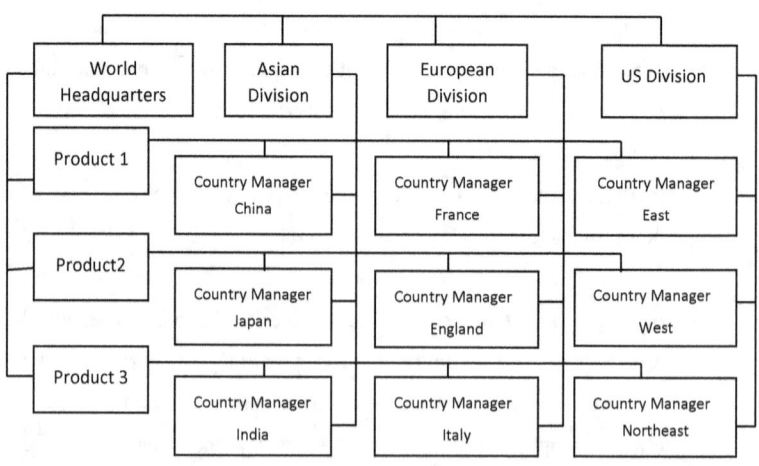

Exhibit 4-4   Worldwide Matrix Structure

4.3 Contrasting Area and Global product Division

Structures

Area and global product division structures can both be appropriate, depending on the objectives a company is trying to achieve. Area structures work best when international sales represent an important percentage of total sales and when the requirements for local responsiveness are high. Global product division structures work best when the number of products the company produces has proliferated and when globalization requirements are high. To establish the contrast more clearly, Exhibit 4-4 summarizes the essential differences between multi-domestic area and global product division structures.

Under the global product division structure, efficient communication of product know-how is maximized. The country manager under a global structure plays more of an administrative-legal role than a strategic one. Not surprisingly the global product structure works best in conditions where product knowledge is more vital than market knowledge. While outputs are tightly controlled, specific operations in any given country may not be well coordinated and there may be some duplication of selling effort. However each product line gets someone's maximum attention.

Under the area division structure, region and country managers are ultimately responsible for corporate strategy in their regions or countries. They have to become familiar with the products and markets of each division. Their task is to adapt corporate strategy to local conditions. Knowledge of local politics, markets, suppliers and channels constitute their distinctive competence. They may not give each product the same degree of effort, but will seek out first their strongest competitive opportunities, i.e., where market demand is highest or competition weakest.

The biggest weaknesses in the global product structure are the growing dependence over time of the affiliates on the parent, and the lack of substantive ideas or initiatives arising from the affiliates. As a result, global product structures are notoriously inflexible. A case in point is Matsushita Electric Industrial, which first introduced a product division structure in 1933. Matsushita's tightly controlled structure was designed to build managerial talent, promote internal competition, and maximize international growth by treating each product division as an independent small business. Overseas marketing affiliates were established, international sales soared, and profits were consolidated on a global basis. By the mid-1980s, Matsushita had emerged as the world's largest producer of consumer electronics. Despite this success, Matsushita has faced serious challenges in the 1990s. Demand for its mainstream color television and VCR products have flattened and profit margins have slipped substantially. Many observers blame Matsushita's once successful product division structure for much of the company's woes. By locating most R&D activities in Japan, Matsushita has missed out on a stream of critical innovations taking place in the United States and Europe. The company has also faced growing demands by host governments for local production and innovation. As technologies such as send-conductors, computers, and robots have blurred, Matsushita's reliance on strictly defined product divisions has only compounded the problems associated with product division inflexibility.

While global product structures have serious shortcomings, area structures may not be the perfect solution. The biggest weakness in the area structure is the difficulty the parent has imposing an overarching strategy on its autonomous affiliates, and hence obtaining some of the benefits of specialization. As a result, area structures are notoriously inefficient. Rather than produce standardized products in world-scale production facilities, area structures mandate smaller plants that are less scale-efficient. Because research and development, purchasing, marketing, and distribution are also duplicated across geographic territories, cumulative overhead costs can be much higher than with most product structures. In an increasingly competitive world, these added costs are often difficult to sustain.

The weaknesses in both the area and product structures are enhanced when a company adopts a structure inconsistent with its international strategy. In other words, if a company has a strategy that emphasizes affiliate input about local markets and yet adopts a global product structure, then lack of affiliate initiative becomes a serious impediment. On the other hand, if a company can increase its efficiency by rearranging its production and standardizing needless differences, but has adopted an area structure, then the autonomy of affiliate managers becomes a serious impediment.

4. 4   The Transnational Option

What should be clear by now is that there can be serious potential problems with both the global product and multi-domestic area structures. With one you get greater global efficiencies and the other, greater local responsiveness. Since there is really no such thing as a perfect organization anyway, one is tempted to suggest simply picking the one closest to the company's product-market thrust and learning to live with the organizational deficiencies. For many companies, that is sound advice. There are, however a number of companies for which these deficiencies are too costly. Telecommunications is a good illustration. Telecommunications companies face powerful pressures toward globalization from high R&D costs and available scale economies, and also powerful pressures toward localization from differences in the systems in place in each country and in the politicization of the industry. Firms facing such challenges sometimes try to capture the benefits of both the global and the multi-domestic structures by developing hybrid structures.

When companies ask, "Isn't there some way to have it all?" the transnational organization and the matrix system have been suggested by some as the solution. The key elements of the transnational structure include a two-way flow of ideas and resources, frequent movement of people between units, extensive use of local boards of directors, and a global perspective on the part of both parent and affiliate. The affiliates of transnational corporations have a good deal more autonomy than those «n global corporations, but still they are an integrated part of a global strategy. In the transnational corporation, initiatives arise in affiliates as well as parents, and inter-affiliate linkages are encouraged. Rather than function as a hierarchy transnational organizations function as a network of horizontal decision-making. Managers make the trade-offs between globalization and localization in the field committed to the corporation and its competitive objectives, and aware of local market anomalies and differences. The organizational challenge is to ensure a continuous supply of such manager over time.

A transnational structure attempts to capture concurrently all of the advantages of area and global product division structures. In order to achieve these dual sets of benefits, the configuration and coordination of activities are mixed; affiliates play leadership roles for some activities and supporting roles for others. Decisions are based on maximizing company skills and competencies, irrespective of activity location or affiliate nationality. To be both efficient and effective, linkages between the company's headquarters and affiliates, as well as across affiliates, are subject to rapid change. As a result, a company with a transnational structure acts essentially as a network of activities with multiple headquarters spread across different countries. Affiliates are given complete control over local products, provide support roles for some global products, and control other global products. Affiliate roles shift over time, and learning and sharing are emphasized. To work effectively, transnational structures emphasize extensive horizontal linkages, effective communication, and extreme flexibility so that companies are able to develop competitive responses not only at head office but in the periphery as well.

4.4.1 Transnational Affiliates and the Development of Mandates

Transnational organizations are designed to concurrently maximize efficiency, local responsiveness, and organizational learning. Affiliates may still manufacture one or two products for world markets, but instead of functioning largely as a factory they handle worldwide responsibilities for other products. In other worlds, the affiliate functions like a domestic product division in some areas while assuming world product mandates in others.

What keeps the affiliate alive as an organism under the transnational structure is direct access to world markets through the development of world product mandates in its area of specialization. World product mandates represent global strategies controlled by the affiliate as opposed to the parent.

In order for a transnational structure to work effectively, affiliates need strong senior managers able to function well among parent company senior managers. If an affiliate becomes a sole or major source of supply and marketing of a specified product area worldwide, its managers soon find themselves operating in the top management committees of the parent organization. The parent has to have confidence in the affiliate's ability to manage its product market and to function effectively within the overall corporate system. As a rule, this means a network of affiliates interchanging sales forces and cross-linking R&D and production facilities.

4.4.2   The Importance of Affiliate Depth and Competence

There is always a danger when recommending strategic initiatives to affiliates if handled badly they can seriously undermine the affiliate's performance and can easily cause a quick exit for both the affiliate and the affiliate general manager. For example, no affiliate is going to be successful in making a major acquisition without its parent's approval. The reality is that in some areas of activity affiliate initiative is more acceptable than in others.

Affiliate managers, whether taking strategic initiative or following parent instructions, absolutely have to be well plugged-in at headquarters. It is not a good idea to presume the competence level of the parent in a given product area, one has to know at the same time, it is not a good idea to make an acquisition or take a strategic initiative without prior parent approval. Taking initiative is not the same as declaring independence. It is independence that is needed, and interdependence requires a measure of integration and working together. Taking the initiative in an interdependent relationship means bringing ideas and plans to the key management committees and championing them. Success is achieved through the quality of the ideas and through the competence with which they are expressed, but also through the preconditioning of other executives present. That is why it is essential for affiliate managers to be well plugged-in at headquarters. They need to understand the mind-set of the other executives and they need opportunities to influence it.

4.4.3   Challenges with Developing Transnational Structures

Managing under multiple mandates is difficult. Most managers can be clarity and exactness in roles and measurements. In ABB's case, for example, each of its 36 business area managers acts in many ways like an air traffic controller. They know where they want the businesses to go and they can set the flight plans, but the country managers ultimately act as pilots. Some may deviate from the plan; some may not be listening. It is not a job for the faint-hearted. To run smoothly the transnational organization requires managers to work toward the benefit of the corporation as a whole. At a time when many companies are shedding employees, it is often difficult to ask employees to think first of the corporation. Transnational corporations that concurrently pursue global efficiencies and local responsiveness risk doing neither well. Affiliates remain suspicious of each other, and many product manages, despite pleas to think globally, continue to favor home country employees and markets. As a result, the transition to a transnational organization is inherently bumpy.

Because of the difficulties of effective implementation, the transnational structure has been proposed as more of an idealized form than a reality. The problem is ultimately one of definition. The transnational structure theoretically achieves the optimal blend of global efficiency and local responsiveness. But these descriptive statements do not constitute a definition of the transnational structure. How does a firm know when it has one? For some, the presence of a shared responsibility matrix structure is the best evidence. In such a structure, geographic areas and product divisions share responsibility for affiliate decisions. The idea is that by sharing the responsibility one forces a constructive dialogue through which the best decision emerges. In this sense, the best decision is one that balances the need for local adaptation with the need for global efficiency. Since the optimal balance is subjective and is constantly shifting, it is difficult for a firm to know whether it has achieved it regardless of the structure it follows. Furthermore, people's egos sometimes get in the way and the matrix structure often fails to achieve its purpose. It is entirely possible to have a transnational perspective without a matrix structure. One simply finds a way to put the matrix mentality into the heads of country managers, or of product division managers, as the case may be. This may ultimately be the managerial challenge of the last half of the 1990s.

Chapter 5
Intra-Company Trade and Transfer Pricing

5.1   Intra-Company Trade

In the global world there is intra-company trade or in house trading. This is trading between mother and daughter companies. It is not the government who decides. Intra-company trade plays a critical role in the operations of transnational companies. It may help a TNC to reduce costs, such as the distribution of goods or acquisition of inputs abroad, or it may help integrate production processes on a global scale. Intra-company trade may respond differently to changes in economic conditions than trade between unrelated parties. For example, it may —at least in the short term — be more insulated from competitive forces in certain markets, or from overall changes in prices, exchange rates, or general economic conditions. Furthermore, prices that govern intra-company trade— often termed "transfer prices — may have their own unique characteristics and determinants.

Statistics on intra-company trade are largely missing. An exception is the United States, which is the home country of most of the world's largest TNCs. The Bureau of Economic Analysis (BEA) has detailed statistics on US TNCs, operations and on foreign TNCs operations in the US, including intra-company trade.

5.2   Intra-Company Trade in America
5.2.1   Value of Intra-Company Trade of United States TNCs and Foreign TNCs in United States

Although fluctuating moderately during the past two decades, the share of intra-company trade—both by United States TNCs and by foreign TNCs—in US exports and imports of goods have changed very little. For both exports and imports, intra-company trade has mainly consisted of shipments from parents to their affiliates, rather than shipments from affiliates to their parent companies. This trend is for both US and foreign TNCs. (BEA, United States Intra-company Trade in Goods)

The proportion in total imports of goods to the United States that is accounted for by intra-company imports of US TNCs has consistently been smaller than the corresponding share of exports. Intra-company exports of United States TNCs have accounted for 21 -26% of total United States exports of goods, while imports have accounted for 15~18%.

The US intra-company exports of foreign TNCs have accounted for about 10% of total US goods exports since 1977; this share has fluctuated between 7% and 12%. The US intra-company imports of foreign TNCs have accounted for a much larger share of total Untied States goods imports since 1977- about 20% or more. The share of imports increased substantially in 1984--1990 from 21% to 28%. Like exports, a very large proportion of the US intra-company imports of foreign TNCs have been accounted for by Japanese-owned affiliates.

5.2.2   Value of Trade Associated with United Slates TNCs

In 1995, trade associated with US TNCs—trade involving United States parents, their foreign affiliates, or both — accounted for 62% of all US exports of goods and for 39% of all US imports of goods. A substantial share of the remaining US exports and imports of goods is associated with affiliates of foreign companies in the United States. In 1995, 23% of US exports of goods and 34% of US imports of goods were associated with such affiliates.

The share in total US exports and imports accounted for by TNCs — both associated and intra-company trade — has changed very little. Associated exports of TNCs declined from 77% in 1982 to 62% in 1995. Associated imports declined from 50% in 1982 to 39% in 1995.

Of the $363 billion in exports of goods associated with US TNCs, 41 % represented trade between US parents and their foreign affiliates (intra-TNC trade), while 59% represented trade with other parties. Of the $213 billion in trade with other parties, 88% were exports shipped by US TNCs to foreigners other than their foreign affiliates, and 12% were exports shipped to foreign affiliates by entities in the US other than their parent organizations.

Of the $288 billion in imports of goods associated with US TNCs, 44% represented intra-company trade, and 56% represented TNC trade with other parties. Of the $163 billion in trade with other parties, 83% were imports shipped to US TNCs by foreigners other than their foreign affiliates, and 17% were imports shipped by foreign affiliates to entities in the US other than their parent organizations.

5.2.3 Composition of Intra-Company Trade

The intra-company trading patterns of US and of foreign TNCs in the United States are fundamentally different in terms of form and industry compositor. The intra-company trade of US TNCs reflects an international division of manufacturing production between affiliated parts of the TNC. For both exports and imports, most of this trade is between United States manufacturing parents and their foreign manufacturing affiliates. The intra-company exports to these manufacturing affiliates have mainly consisted of materials and components for further processing or assembly.

In contrast, the intra-company trade in the United States of foreign TNCs is largely connected with distribution and marketing activities. For both exports and imports, US wholesale trade affiliates account for most of this trade. Imports by these affiliates from their foreign parent organizations consist almost exclusively of finished goods for resale.

(Data on the intended use of exports by these affiliates are not available.)

5.2.4 Intra-Company Trade's Relation to Trade Partners Income Level

Intra-company transactions-particularly shipments flowing from parent companies to their affiliates-tend to be relatively more important in US trade with higher-income countries. Among 59 major US trading partners, there is a pronounced tendency for the proportion both of intra-company exports of US TNCs in total exports and of intra-company imports of foreign TNCs in total imports to increase with the per-capita gross national product (GNP) of the trading partner. The average share of US exports accounted for by intra-company trade of US TNCs increases from 4% for the 11 trading partners with per-capita GNP of less than $1,000, to 23% for the 14 trading partners with per-capita GNP of $20,000 or more. The average share of US imports accounted for by intra-company trade increases from less than 3% for the 11 countries with the lowest per-capita GNP, to 35% for the 14 countries with the highest per-capita GNP.

5.3   Transfer Pricing
5.3.1   What's Transfer Price

When parent company, or one part of a transnational organization in one country transfers (that is, sells) goods, services or know-how to another part in another country, the price charged for these goods or services is called * transfer price' It is the price of in house trading. These costs are not documented openly. Therefore if the situation is difficult in one country then the cost can be adjusted. You can lower your business costs significantly by putting into place an efficient transfer pricing policy. This may be a purely arbitrary figure, meaning by this that it may be unrelated to costs incurred, may be unrelated to operations carried out or to added value. Transfer price can be set at a level which reduces or even cancels out the total tax which has to be paid by the transnational corporation.

5.3.2 How Does Transfer Price Reduce the Total Tax Burden

Consider ourselves to be directors of the TNC. We are sitting in its boardroom at the head office in the home country of the TNC. The Finance Director is reviewing our operations. He is talking about our trade with another company in another country. We are the parent company. They are one of our subsidiary companies. This means that they belong to us, that in the end we decide what they do and do not do, what happens to their profits. We the parent company, are located in the 'home country'. The subsidiary company is located in another country, namely in the "host country". The Finance Director is simplifying the picture for our benefit.

1. Paying Some Tax
Case A

The subsidiary company buys goods at $100 each. They repack them and then export them from their country to our country, selling them to us at a price of $200 each.

They are transferring them to us for a transfer price of $200. So they have made a profit of 200 -100 = $100 and we are getting them at a price of S200. Having imported them at $200 each we sell them for $300 and thus make a profit of 300 -200 =$100. Our overall profit is thus $100 in the subsidiary company's host country and another $100 in the TNC's country, a total of $200.

However, we need to consider thetax   these   companies have to pay on their profits, as the rates of tax (company or corporation tax) is different in the two countries. The subsidiary has to pay corporation tax of 20% of the $100 profit and so the tax amounts to $20. Our home-country corporation tax is 60% of the $100 profit, and so our tax amounts to $60. Overall, tax paid is 20 +60 = 80 and this reduces our before-tax profit of $200 to an after-tax profit of 200-80 =120. The subsidiary contributed $80 to this profit, while our own operations contributed $40. The after-tax profit generated by us, that is by the parent company in the home country, was smaller because we paid corporation tax of 60% which compares with the subsidiary's 20%.

Our Finance Director points out that as the overall after-tax profit is 40% of the selling price we should be pleased with the outcome. However, we can tell the subsidiary what to charge and can make the transfer price whatever we like. The transfer price is arbitrary, depending as it does only on agreement between ourselves and the subsidiary, and thus on ourselves.

Case B

The transfer price is now $280. This has the effect of shifting before-tax profits from the parent company's home country (corporation tax 60%) to the subsidiary s host country (corporation tax 20%). Overall, we now pay less tax (36+12=48) and as the before-tax profit is unchanged ($200), the after-tax profit becomes 200 -48 =152 and that is much more than the corresponding profit of $120 we made with a transfer price of $200. The subsidiary contributes $144 to this while our own contribution is $8. Our overall after-tax profit is now 51 % of the selling price.

Merely by changing the transfer price to an arbitrary higher figure of $280 we have increased our overall after-tax profit from $120 to $152, increased it by a staggering

27%.

2. Paying No Tax
Case C

As the transfer price is arbitrary, it can be $300. This means that we are buying and selling at the same price of $300. Overall tax paid is now $40 and our after-tax profit becomes $160. The subsidiary contributes $160 to this while our own contribution is 0. So what we have done is to shift all our profits to the subsidiary and do not need to pay tax in the home country. But we need not stop there. The parent company can shift even more of its profits to the subsidiary. It can make a loss and this is illustrated by Case D.

3. Getting Tax Repaying
Case D

This case shows what happens if the transfer price is increased to $400. The subsidiary makes a profit of S300 and we make a loss of $100 on each item. This loss can be used by us to reduce our tax liability on other profitable operations carried out by the parent company in the home country. As a result we pay correspondingly less tax. The subsidiary pays corporation tax of $60 on their profits while we, the parent company, reduce our tax bill by $60, in effect getting a rebate of $60. Hence the overall result is that we pay no tax at all on this transaction and our after-tax profit becomes $200. We can take this one step further and make the Transfer Price $500 (see Case E).

Case E

The subsidiary now makes a profit of $400 and we make a

loss of $200. The subsidiary pays corporation tax of $80 on their profits while we, the parent company, reduce our tax bill by $120, in effect getting a rebate of $120. Hence the overall result is we get a tax rebate of $120 in the home country, pay $80 corporation tax in the host country, and are thus left with a tax rebate of $40 on this transaction. Adding this to our profit increases the after-tax profit from $200 to $240.

5.3.3   Tax Avoidance
1.   Tax Avoidance Increases Profits
So by increasing the purely arbitrary transfer price we doubled our after-tax profit, increasing it by 100%. This was done without any change to our procedures, operations or added value, was done by merely changing book entries. So where do these additional profits come from? They arise from tax avoidance. In other words it is possible for a transnational company to minimize its liability for corporation tax by transfer pricing.

This is legal until governments legislate to prevent this practice. But note that in the cases we discussed, the tax paid to the host-country government increased, while the tax paid to the home-country government decreased, case by case. In other words, one government's loss is the other government's gain. So one government can be expected to want to legislate against unfair transfer pricing practices, while the other government can be expected to object to, and to resist, such legislation.

2. Tax Avoidance Transfers The Tax Obligation
The parent company operates in the home country. The government of that country or state spends money on

behalf of its citizens-providing education, health care, social security, protection against crime and security against attack from outside. It collects much of the money it needs from citizens and companies by means of a tax on income -- those who earn most pay most, those who earn least pay least. This tax is called Corporation Tax when it is collected from companies (corporations) and Income Tax when it is collected from individuals.

Say a transnational corporation has increased its profits by tax avoidance. As the government's expenses have not changed it must make up this shortfall elsewhere. From its other tax payers, say from its citizens. So its citizens pay more tax, the government can now spend the same amount as before, the TNC's profits have increased. In other words, the TNC's increased profits arise from money which is in effect collected by the government by taxation from its taxpayers. The TNC, and this means the owners and directors of the TNC, are thus in effect taxing the people and in this way increasing the TNC s profits and thus their own incomes and wealth. A matter far removed from earning reasonable profits from providing needed quality goods and services at reasonable prices in open competition with other corporations.

Many TNCs have grown to a size where they threaten or dominate the economic and financial independence and well-being of many countries TNCs are accountable to their directors and owners for profitability and growth instead of being accountable to elected representatives of the people for acting for or against the national interest. That TNCs can gain so much profit from tax avoidance, which is from in effect taxing the population, is a case in point. TNCs need to be made accountable to elected representatives of the people, for their policies and for acting for or against the national interest.

5.4   Tax   Havens   and   the   Transnational Corporation

A perennial charge against the transnational corporation is its use (or misuse) of tax havens to shield income from the local tax collector. Tax-haven countries include those countries whose moderate level of taxation and liberal tax incentives enable the transnational corporation to substantially reduce or defer taxation on income channeled through these countries.

5.4.1   Types of Tax Havens

The various tax havens of the world can be grouped into four types:

Type 1:   Tax havens that have no income or capital gains tax or gift and estate tax

Type 2:   Tax havens that do impose taxes, but whose rate is very low

Type 3:   Tax havens that tax income from domestic sources but exempt all income from foreign sources

Type 4:   Countries that allow special tax privileges and are suitable for tax havens only for selected purposes

The first group encompasses many of the tax havens in the Caribbean, such as the Bahamas. Bermuda, and the Cayman Islands. The Bahamas levies a small tax of $100 per year on all Bahamian companies. It has no tax treaty with any country requiring it to furnish information to other countries. Since 1960, manufacturing companies have been getting long-term guarantees against taxes. Bermuda has no tax treaties and has moderate corporate and incorporation fees. In the Cayman Islands, foreign-owned companies are guaranteed against taxes for 20 years, and the Cayman Islands has no tax treaties and has moderate corporate and incorporation fees.

A country representative of the second group would be the British Virgin Islands because of its 12% income tax rate. However, the British Virgin Islands' usefulness as a tax haven in relation to other countries is somewhat diminished by its 12% withholding tax on dividends. Another major tax haven is the Netherlands Antilles, a colony of the Netherlands located a few miles off the coast of Venezuela. Most business is centered in Curacao. Income taxes are very low, and there are special tax privileges to shipping, aviation, and holding companies.

A country whose tax benefits are characteristic of the third group is Hong Kong. Although Hong Kong imposes a nominal tax of 15% on Hong Kong-sourced income, foreign-sourced income is completely exempt. Nor is there any tax on capital, capital gains, or dividends remitted to foreign shareholders Another popular country under this group is Panama, which has a tax on domestically sourced income but none on foreign-sourced income of companies is located in Panama. It also has no income tax treaties and encourages incorporation in Panama trough very liberal incorporation laws that allow the articles of incorporation to be written in any language. Panama's role as a secure tax haven, however, has been diminished by the political unrest in that country.

The fourth group mainly includes those countries that are trying to promote development in certain regions or encourage industrialization within the country. The most notable example here is the Republic of Ireland, which ex-

72

empts from taxation the export earnings of corporations that set up manufacturing operations in certain regions. Also included in this group is Puerto Rico, which grants tax ex- emption for up to 17 years for firms to set up operations in certain less-developed zones.

There are a few European tax-haven countries that should be mentioned: Switzerland, the Netherlands, and Liechtenstein. Switzerland has some unique enticements for the tax avoider. First, t does not tax profits that locally incorporated businesses earn outside the country. However, Switzerland has a decentralized government consisting of 25 sovereign cantons, and most direct taxes are levied by the cantons and not the federal government. The cantons do impose a nominal tax on capital. Second, Swiss laws allow corporations extraordinary freedom from official surveillance. Tax evasion is not a criminal offense in Switzerland, and even the Swiss federal tax authorities know that local banks will refuse their requests for information.

The Netherlands is a favorite tax haven for holding companies. A holding company in the Netherlands does not pay any tax on income and capital gains emanating from its direct (not portfolio) participations in either domestic or foreign subsidiaries. Moreover, the tax treaties that the Netherlands has with other countries almost eliminate the withholding tax on dividend distributions to the parent company.

Liechtenstein is a tiny principality that is tucked pic- turesquely in the Alpine scenery; it has 20,000 people, 7,000 cows, and about 15,000 "foreign legal entities." These entities are companies, partnerships, and other vehicles through which foreigners can hide their money, free of virtually all taxes and safe from anybody's curiosity. The most famous Liechtenstein corporate device is the Anstalt — a company that can be used for virtually any purpose. Its only visibility is on the public register, which merely gives the Anstalt's name, capital at formation, and the name of its Liechtenstein representative — by law there must be at least one resident Liechtensteiner on the board.

5.4.2   How to Select the Type of Tax Haven

Before selecting the type of tax haven to use, the TNC must develop a framework to evaluate its projected needs against the advantages of the various tax havens. Factors that are usually considered in choosing a tax haven include the following:

(1)   The political and economic stability of the country and the integrity of its government

(2)   The attitude of the country toward tax-haven business

(3)   The other taxes, aside from income taxes, it imposes

(4)   Tax treaties (Some tax havens owe their very existence to the fact that they are parties to advantageous tax --- treaty arrangements. Other tax-haven countries are party to few, if any, tax treaties)

(5)   The lack of exchange controls (Although some tax havens have exchange controls, most offshore companies organized by nonresidents are granted relative freedom from such controls.)

(6)   Liberal incorporations laws that minimize both the cost of incorporation and the length of time it takes to incorporate

(7)   Banking facilities

(8)   Transportation facilities and telephone, cable, and telex communications with the rest of the world

(9)   The long-range prospects for continued freedom from taxation

After the selection of a tax haven, the next relevant consideration is the form of organization. This choice entails the branch versus subsidiary decision, as well as the use of any tax-incentive organization (for example, a possessions corporation). Three key factors underlie this decision about the form of organization.

The first factor is the projected cash flows in the country under consideration. A forecast of several years of initial operating losses in any country would be significant in weighing the desirability of operating initially as a branch. The second factor is the attitude of the U. S. parent corporation toward repatriation of funds. The tax-free use of funds can be an important factor in the determination of working-capital needs. Also, earnings allowed to accumulate offshore may be repatriated tax free if certain forms of organization that allow for tax-free liquidation are undertaken. The third factor to consider is alternative uses for funds. If the parent company has other offshore facilities, the earnings from some facilities can provide cash flows for other subsidiaries. This factor is especially important for a parent that is constantly seeking out and developing new foreign investment opportunities.

With the preceding considerations and factors in mind, the TNC can make a selective examination of possible locations. The focus here is on the relative advantages and disadvantages of each country on the basis of its tax laws. The objective of tax planning is to interpret laws correctly to legally avoid paying unnecessary taxes, rather than to escape corporate obligations under the law.

Chapter 6
Strategies of Transnational Corporations

6. 1 Traditional Method of Strategy Formulation

A great deal must be learned about an organization so that strategy formulation decisions can be based upon appropriate information. It almost goes without saying that strategists must understand all there is to know about the internal operations of an organization before strategy can be effectively formulated and implemented. The external influences acting on the firm also must be analyzed, documented, and understood to manage the strategy process effectively.

6.1.1 Environmental Analysis

The dimensions of environment can be generally classified by a set of key factors that describe the economic, political/legal, technological, and social surroundings. These, in turn, can be overlaid by the various constituents of the firm, including shareholders, customers, competitors, suppliers, employees and the general public. To assess environmental conditions, concern is focused on opportunities and threats that exist, or may arise, through impacts on and by the firm's constituents.

6.1.2 Industry Analysis

Industry analysis complements analyses of the other dimensions of a firm's environment. It focuses on the industries in which the firm competes. The breadth and depth of industry analysis and the boundaries for information gathering are defined by these industries. Thus industry analysis involves the same processes as those identified earlier for environmental analysis, except that it logically must be preceded by identification of the appropriate industries for analysis along with descriptions of the various characteristics of those industries.

Industry analysis is relevant in any of these situations: 1) The firm's strategy defines the business in terms of specific industries. 2) The firm is facing new forms of extra-industry competition. 3) The firm is contemplating entry into a new industry.

Michael E Porter developed an assessment model, called "Five Forces Model of Competition" for analyzing industry structure that focuses on the forces imposed on the process of competing by five influences: The intensity of rivalry among competitors, the threat of new entrants, the threat of substitute products, the bargaining power of suppliers, and the bargaining power of buyers or customers. Some environmental influences affect a firm through the industries in which it competes. These influences, the nature of their present and future effects on the appropriate industries, and characteristics of the relationships between the firm's relevant industries and the firm itself are the subjects of industry analysis. Industry analysis focuses interest on two primary levels: The structure and performance of the industry as a whole; The strategies and performance of individual competitors.

6.1.3 Financial Analysis

Financial statements can reveal much about a firm's operating strengths and weaknesses. They also serve as a basis for predicting future financial developments. To the extent that the performance of a parts of an organization is ultimately reflected in the magnitude of entries in a firm's financial statements, financial analysis can structure or bound the question of now we a strategy is working.

Comprehensive financial analysis consists of four elements: ratio analysis of the firm's historical financial performance, interpretation of each cash flow position, analysis of retained earnings position, and predictions of future financial statements.

6.1.4 Internal Diagnosis

Most strategic operating characteristics are manifested either directly or indirectly as symptoms in a firm's financial statements. These symptoms must be "dug out" of the statements and then interpreted in operational terms for strategic analysis to begin. Through the interpretation of operational causes of financial symptoms, the strategist can identify many of the firm's strengths and weaknesses. But, as Berg has noted, "There is a temptation to spend too much time on the analysis of financial performance and position..... and not enough time on the more difficult analysis of the underlying factors....". These underlying factors are usually the strengths and weaknesses uncovered during analysis of other functional areas. In other words, financial analysis can reveal symptoms of problems or evidence of strengths in the other functional areas.

Therefore, financial analysis can be viewed as a way to

uncover questions about performance, to which the answers are likely to be found by analysis of other functional areas. For example, if financial analysis showed relatively high gross profits for a firm experiencing declining sales, the analyst would probably turn to either its marketing function (to determine if prices charged by the firm were too high) or its production systems (to see if raw materials inventory costs were leading to excessive cost of goods sold). There are two fundamental ways to conduct an internal analysis: vertical and horizontal. For the vertical approach, strengths and weaknesses are identified at each organizational level. The horizontal analysis corresponds to the functional areas. Strengths and weaknesses are identified for each function. We prefer the horizontal approach because it seems to be more universally applicable. Analysis can be focused on function departments, or whatever basis of departmentalization has been used a particular organization.

Stevenson found that managers seem to use three types of criteria in identifying strengths and weaknesses: historical, competitive, and normative. Analyzing functional areas by historical criteria means comparing present values with their historical counterparts and identifying strengths and weaknesses on the basis of those comparisons. Competitive comparisons involve assessing similarities and dissimilarities with successful competitors and finding strengths and weaknesses accordingly. Similarly normative comparisons are those where present characteristics are compared with ideal values as perceived by the analyst or an expert opinion.

Together these four analytical activities — environmental, industry, and financial analysis and internal diagnosis of functional areas — are undertaken to generate a data set consisting of strengths, weaknesses, threats, and opportunities that comprehensively describes the internal and external characteristics of the organization. This information is then used as input to the strategy formulation process.

6.2   Basic   Strategies   for   Transnational Corporations

It is in determining how to compete that most TNCs have run into problems. TNCs in the late 1990s are confronted with a bewildering array of strategy options. Most TNCs conceptualize strategy as a hierarchy that includes both corporate-level strategies and business-unit-level strate-gies. Corporate strategies typically focus on two things: (I) determining the industries in which the TNC will compete, and (2) determining how the various businesses within the INC will coordinate activities. Business-unit strategies focus on market share battles through competitive and international Positioning. Business-unit managers rather than corporate executives have become the primary drivers of international strategy.

TNCs use many of the same strategies practiced by domestic companies. There are three basic strategies: generic, competitive, and diversification. Like solely domestic firms, transnational corporations use these strategies to achieve and maintain competitive advantages over rivals.

6.2.1   Generic Strategy

Generic strategies represent very basic ways that both domestic and transnational companies keep and achieve competitive advantage. Porter identifies the two primary generic strategies that companies use to gain competitive advantage: differentiation and low cost.

Companies that adopt a differentiation strategy find ways to provide   superior value to customers. Superior value comes from sources such as exceptional product quality, unique product features, or high-quality service. High quality; service, or other unique characteristics of a differentiated product usually increase costs. Consequently, to provide a good profit margin, the differentiating company must charge higher prices to offset its additional costs. Differentiation leads to higher profits because people will often pay a higher price for the extra value provided by the superior product or service.

Companies that adopt a low-cost strategy produce or deliver products or services equal to those of their competitors. However, low-cost companies find the means to produce their products or to deliver their services more efficiently than the competition. That is, they lower the costs of their products without sacrificing on what the customers' desire. The cost savings that improve efficiency may occur anywhere from the creation.pf the product to its final sale.

6.2.2   Competitive Strategy

Besides using the basic generic strategies in their oper-ations, transnational corporations use several strategic moves called competitive strategies. Competitive strategies can be offensive or defensive. In offensive strategies, companies directly target rivals from whom they wish to capture market share. Examples of offensive competitive strategies include direct attacks, end-run offensive, preemptive strategies, and acquisitions. Usually, transnational managers analyze the strengths and weaknesses of their competitors separately in each country. Different countries represent different markets and often require different attack strategies. In a competitive industry, all managers should expect attacks from rival firms. To counteract these attacks, companies use defensive competitive strategies. In defensive strategies, companies seek to beat back or discourage the offensive strategies of rivals.

6.2.3   Diversification Strategy

When a company moves from a single type of business into two or more businesses, this is called diversification strategy. There are two basic types of diversification: related and unrelated. In related diversification, companies start or acquire businesses that are similar in some way to their original or core business. In unrelated diversification, firms acquire businesses in any industry. The main concern is whether a business represents a good financial investment. Experts do not agree on which form of diversification is best for transnational corporations. The related diversifiers better positioned to take advantage of economies of scale and business similarities, and unrelated diversifiers can seek growth industries in attractive countries.

6.3   Multi-domestic Strategy and Global Strategy

A fundamental strategic dilemma faced by all transnational corporations is how to compete internationally. Should the company emphasize responding to differences in the markets in all the countries in which it operates? If the answer is yes, this is called the multi-domestic strategy. Or, should the company de-emphasize local differences and conduct business similarly throughout the world? If so, this is called the global strategy.

6.3.1   Multi-domestic Strategy

Companies that lean toward the multi-domestic strategy stress customizing their organizations and products to country or regional differences. The focus is on satisfying local customer needs by tailoring products or services to meet those needs. Forces that suggest a multi-domestic strategy come primarily from national or cultural differences in costumer tastes and variations in customer needs. In addition, national differences in how industries work and in political pressures can lead companies to favor local responsiveness. For example, government regulations can require a company to share ownership with a local company. Some governments also require companies to produce their products in the countries in which they sell.

Businesses pursuing multi-domestic strategies first develop products for their home market and then offer them for sale or adaptation by their overseas affiliates. Affiliates are developed with the capacity to absorb parent company technology and adapt the resulting products to local conditions and tastes. Traditionally, multi-domestic affiliates manufacture products for their own national markets, adapting the parent company product line as required. If specialization is at the heart of global strategies, duplication and autonomy are at the heart of multi-domestic strategies. In the pure multi-domestic model, it is technology and skills that cross national boundaries, not products.

Historically, the U.S. and TNCs have approached international competition by pursuing multi-domestic strategies. Multi-domestic strategies are designed to maximize the local responsiveness of businesses. Encouraged by historically fragmented European markets, and cultures that readily accommodated the delegation of decision making to overseas managers, the U.S. and European TNCs achieved major successes in international markets in the 1960s and 1970s by emphasizing multi-domestic strategies. However, with the emergence of the first strains of globalization pressures in the 1970s, multi-domestic strategies began to falter in many industries. As industry pressures began to take on more global dimensions, it became possible for business to gain a competitive advantage by pursuing global strategies.

6.3.2   Global Strategy

Transnational companies that lean toward a global solution, at least to the largest degree possible, reduce costs by using standardized products, promotional strategies, and distribution channels in every country. In addition, the globally oriented transnational companies seek sources of lower costs or higher quality anywhere in their value chain and anywhere in the world. For example, in such companies, headquarters, R&D, production, or distribution centers may be located anywhere they can provide the best value added with quality or lower cost.

Under a global strategy, businesses focus on maximizes international efficiency by locating activities in low-cost countries, producing standardized products from world-scale facilities, globally integrating operations, and subsidizing intra-country market share battles. Global businesses conceive and design products for world markets from the outset. Frequently, affiliates in key markets have input into product design, but once the parent organization launches a new product, the affiliate's role reverts to that of implementer.

Global products are usually marketed to international similarities rather than to cultural differences, and marketing strategies are therefore established as a rule in the parent organization. Products are manufactured wherever in the world the necessary quality standards can be achieved at the lowest cost, including transportation to key markets. As a practical matter, large markets attract production because market share is often enhanced by the presence of a production facility. Also host country governments sometimes induce local production through non-tariff barriers to trade, but the classic global strategy is conceived without artificial impediments to the movement of goods.

Chapter 7
International Strategic Alliances

7. 1   Conception of Strategic Alliances

Webster's dictionary defines strategic as "important" and alliance as "association of interests". "Strategic alliances, then, are associations important to alliance partners and formed to further their common interests. They can involve franchising and licensing agreements, partnership contracts, equity investments in new or existing joint ventures and consortia.

Strategic alliances are well-known tools available to, and used by, transnational corporation managers. For example, of the more than 167,000 foreign-funded investments in China in the mid-1990s, the 64% were joint ventures and 15% were cooperative partnerships. In the auto industry, more than 1000 alliances have been created worldwide; in the airline industry, the number exceeds 300. Strategic alliances have proven to be important to both domestic and multinational business, as well as to the economies of the countries involved.

The term 'strategic alliance' is used to describe a wide range of cooperative partnerships and joint ventures. Strategic alliances have three distinguishing characteristics: (1) Two or more entities unite to pursue a set of important, agreed-upon goals while in some way remaining independent subsequent to the formation of an alliance; (2) The partners share both the benefits of the alliance and control over the performance of assigned tasks during the line of the alliance. This is the most distinctive characteristic of alliances and the one that makes them so difficult to manage; (3) The partners contribute on a continuing basis in one or more key strategic (that is. important to them) areas, for example, technology or products.

Many kinds of alliances exist and there are many ways to manage them. In addition, when these alliances cross national borders, cross-cultural complexities impact on their effectiveness. An alliance's success, therefore, is highly dependent on contingent thinking and entrepreneurial skills.

7.2 Kinds of Strategic Alliances

Alliances can involve substantial investments in joint ventures. For example, in 1997 British Petroleum (BP) joined with Mobil Oil in a refining, distribution and marketing joint venture, a $5.00 billion organization. The two companies, which were not in themselves market leaders, expected to gain scale benefits and scale economics. Strategic alliances also include cooperative partnerships. International airline alliances, such as the one proposed between British Airways (BA) and American Airlines (AA) in 1998 involving operational and sales activities, are a familiar of alliance partnership which does not involve equity investment. British Airways also is involved in several continuing franchise partner- ships, some of which involve equity investments.

Governments worldwide encourage and stimulate strategic alliance. Government interest in joint ventures is one of the major drivers that encourage domestic and multinational businesses to enter strategic alliances. In cooperation with transnational corporations, governments use strategic alliances in many ways:

(1)   To privatize state-owned companies while continuing to profit from and to some degree control the businesses

(2)   To attract capital while nurturing local businesses

(3)   To bring technology to their country

(4)   To improve overall economic performance quickly, especially in developing countries, without entirely relin- quishing control of local businesses to foreign operators.

Understanding strategic alliances also requires understanding what they are not. Because they do not involve two or more independent firms sharing benefits and control over a continuing time period, mergers and acquisitions are not considered strategic alliances, nor are wholly-owned subsidiaries of multinational corporations. Joint ventures also may or may not be true strategic alliances, depending on the circumstances. For example, the Fuji Photo Film Company brought little to the Fuji-Xerox joint venture in Japan beyond its initial capital contribution. The venture functioned as a relatively independent subsidiary of Xerox because Fuji did not have access to the technology and contributed no technology of its own. As a result, this joint venture only nominally can be considered a strategic alliance. An agreement through which a firm grants a license for using technology in exchange for a royalty also is not considered a strategic alliance except when there is continuing contribution and control among two or more independent firms.

7.3   Why Strategic Alliances

Strategic alliances appeal to transnational corporations for reasons other than because many countries require foreign investors to use them. If planned and managed effectively, they can:

(1)   Enable overseas expansion and provide access to new markets

(2)   Add value to a firm's product line

(3)   Expand distribution and provide access to materials

(4)   Develop and improve operations; facilities and processes, and provide access to new capabilities, new knowledge and new technologies

(5)   Provide additional financial resources

(6)　Decrease risks and enable relatively rapid adaptation to changing competitive market forces

(7)　Create new opportunities when faced with intense global competition

(8)　Reduce competition

Strategic alliances often are useful in establishing a comprehensive integrated package of enablers, including marketing and productions, organization, financial and accounting, and telecommunications/information systems operations. These enablers can help companies rapidly penetrate new markets or expand in existing ones. Through an alliance with Mobil, British petroleum was able to establish a strong market position in Europe in 2~3 years. Doing this on their own had been estimated to take 8 years. America Online, Inc. (AOL) used alliances in 1998 to establish a major position in Europe when competing against strongly entrenched telecommunications companies.

Another key trend driving strategic alliance growth is the globalization of business and of knowledge used in business. The importance of Knowledge—in addition to the traditional economic forces of labor, land and capital — to wealth accumulation has received considerable attention recently. The rapidity with which knowledge can be communicated and translated globally into new products and services has contributed to the growing use of strategic alliances in today's highly competitive, global environment.

Strategic alliances also enable adaptation of common global frameworks to diverse local requirements. For example, the Gillette Company markets well-known global brands and products. Gillette has used alliances, especially in the distribution area, to expand rapidly worldwide. Gillette views strategic alliances as an effective way to move quickly into different countries in an adaptive, flexible way, while still retaining global brand identities. Hundreds of other transnational corporations have used strategic alliances to balance and synergistically use local diversity.

Although strategic alliances are an effective management tool, they are not appropriate for all companies or all industry situations. As of 1997, Japan's largest telecommunications operation, Nippon Telegraph and telephone, had developed international markets independently and had shown little interest in joining global telecommunications alliances.

It can help to review the successes and failures of others, and one can learn from one's own and other's experiences, but the experiences of others are rarely formulas that can be directly transferred to managing new situations at different companies, which most often have their own special requirements.

7. 4 Planning and Managing Strategic Alliances

7.4.1 Determining Strategic Fit: Enterprise-Wide Strategic Alignment

Strategic alliances can be a useful method or enabler for multinational growth for many enterprise-wide strategic reasons. For example, airlines use strategic alliances frequently to meet changing worldwide market needs. In September 1995, Delta Air Lines received approval and antitrust immunity to further its partnership with Austrian Airlines, Sabena and Swissair. This partnership was strengthened and expanded in 1997. Similar immunity was also granted to an alliance of United Airlines, Lufthansa, air Canada, Scandinavian airlines and Thai Airways. In addition to permitting the integration of passengers on selected flights, such immunity allows airlines to integrate fight schedules, marketing plans and sales promotions.

Such alliances allow airline partners to function as one major worldwide carrier without investing in one another. The partners remain separate firms and preserve capital. Competing airlines sometimes form alliances, as in early 1997, when Alitalia (Italy) and air France formed a marketing alliance. Such alliances are not always easy to manage, however. Disputes arose in the mid-1990s between KLM and Northwest during their alliance, and many complaints and obstacles have arisen concerning the proposed 1998 British Airways/American airlines partnership.

Automakers have used all kinds of strategic alliances—with suppliers, competitors, non-competitors and potential competitors. For example, Mitsubishi used such ventures to move into Asia ahead of stronger competitors, since it was unable to compete with these entrenched competitors in the US and Japan. In early 1997, Volkswagen (Germany) and General Motors (USA) announced joint venture plans with Finnish, Swedish and central European partners to make cars in Russia.

Strategic alliances do not fit all company strategies. Citibank, for example, has successfully expanded in Asia on its own, both because of the nature of the banking business and because of its supporting computer and telecommunications technologies which enable creating and servicing banking outlets quickly without local partner support. Citibank also has the capital resources to support these moves. Industry, market and company strategic-fit and operational-fit requirements not only dictate the type of strategic alliances used, they also dictate whether or not strategic alliances are needed.

7.4.2 Negotiating Strategic Alliances and Selecting Compatible Partners

The negotiation process for strategic alliances often is complex and lengthy. For example, the process General Motors went through in trying to put together a billion-dollar joint venture in China in the mid-1950s was without a predetermined script and lasted several years.

In 1996, a major chemical company with one joint venture in china in 1996, was planning four more. Based on its experience, the company thought each deal would take at least 2 years to complete. The complexities arose because the deals involved negotiating supply contracts with local companies, upgrading existing facilities, renegotiating labor contracts, complying with international environmental codes and waste disposal regulations and reducing the workforce.

Selecting partners involves matching a company's needs, values and capabilities with those of the partner firm(s) or government body. In addition, an alliance's success may depend on the type of people involved — their personal characteristics, values and capabilities — as well as on the personal chemistry among partners. Some consultants specialize in prescreening individuals to identify the entrepreneurial, forthright, honest, innovative and adaptable characteristics which are likely predictors of effective alliance partners. Observing and gaining insight into the traits of the individuals and firms involved is critical to the partner negotiation and selection process. Personal relations and trust must be cultivated and nurtured to make the alliance a success over the years.

7.4.3 Determining Specific Type and Structure of a Strategic Alliance

Many of the factors discussed in the preceding sections—strategic fit, negotiating processes and partner selection factors—can affect the type and structure of a strategic alliance. Other factors which help determine and develop an effective operational fit through the alliance structure include:

(1)   The type of business — The structural needs of the banking, auto and airline industries differ greatly. Airline alliances are largely co-marketing and co-service partnerships, auto alliances most often involve manufacturing joint ventures, and banking alliances normally involve financial services systems.

(2)   The enterprises involved — The Airbus consortium formed to build jet airliners involved four companies in four different countries with each doing a different part of the manufacturing process, and so required a different structure from that of the government agency.

(3)   The potential for misuse of proprietary knowledge — Gillette imported its advanced technology razor, the Sensor, and manufactured only carbon and steel blades and older razor models in china in order to protect proprietary knowledge.

(4)   The people involved — Special skills requirements and trustworthiness of available local help can affect the management, operational and financial controls built into

the structure.

(5)   The importance of the alliance to each party — A foreign municipality may be interested only in the income from a venture, and not in ways it can provide growth for other related businesses the municipality is involved in. This was the case with Gillette where its joint venture partner retained only a 30% financial interest and did not require interlocking supply contracts. In contrast, a US chemical firm s venture in China used the Chinese partner's manufacturing facilities and had raw material supply contracts with the Chinese firm's other plants.

(6)   Potential rivalry — The benefits of the learning potential in the General Motors alliance with Toyota in Fremont, California, apparently outweighed the fact that the automobiles produced were to be sold competitively under both the General Motors and Toyota brands. The deal was structured to terminate in the 1990s in order to tailor the structure to the logical time limits of the learning benefits.

Developing detailed alliance structures involves defining: percentage of ownership; mix of financing; kinds of material, technology, and machinery to be contributed by each partner; division and sharing of activities; staffing; location; autonomy; controls (not just for operations but also for measuring and controlling each partner's contributions over time); and guidelines for management after alliance inception.

The best structure is the organizational arrangement which most effectively meets strategic fit, operational fit and personal chemistry situation requirements and which is accepted through negotiation by all parties concerned. Negotiators should be convinced that the structure will enable both parties to improve their chances of obtaining the desired benefits from the relationship. The alliance must fulfill four basic criteria for each partner: it must add value, enable learning, protect and enhance core competencies and competitive advantages, and enable the operational flexibility needed for the venture to be successful.

7.4.4 Making Multinational Strategic Alliances Work: Leading and Managing

Managing and leading strategic alliances involves doing whatever is necessary to get the job done, within well-defined strategic frameworks. This task often involves reconciling and balancing diverse, conflicting and often paradoxical forces on a continuing basis in a complex and rapidly changing environment.

The tasks include staffing decisions, for example, the balance between expatriate and local management. Solutions depend on such situational factors as the nature of the product and business, competitive market pressures, available personnel, alliance partner relationships and their respective strategic goals, country cultures involved, local laws and regulations, and existing pay scales. Other tasks include managing cultural differences, developing organization structures, personnel administration, monitoring on a continuing bass and coordinating strategic alliance and home country operations.

(The End)

www.ingramcontent.com/pod-product-compliance
Lightning Source LLC
Chambersburg PA
CBHW052333220526
45472CB00001B/399

* 9 7 8 1 9 8 1 2 3 4 1 9 6 *